COMPLETE POEMS

Salvatore Quasimodo

COMPLETE POEMS

introduced and translated by

JACK BEVAN

CARCANET CLASSICS

First published in 1983 by Anvil Poetry Ltd
This edition published in 2021 by
Carcanet
Alliance House, 30 Cross Street
Manchester M2 7AQ
www.carcanet.co.uk

Introduction and translations © Jack Bevan 1983, 2021
Original texts are from
Tutte le poesie © Arnoldo Mondadori Editore 1960
Dare e avere © Arnoldo Mondadori Editore 1966

The right of Jack Bevan to be identified as the translator
of this work has been asserted in accordance with the Copyright,
Designs and Patents Act of 1988.

A CIP catalogue record for this book is
available from the British Library.

ISBN 978 1 80017 108 4

Printed in Great Britain by SRP Ltd, Exeter, Devon

The publisher acknowledges financial
assistance from Arts Council England.

For Colleen

costei per fermo nacque in Paradiso!

J. B.

ACKNOWLEDGEMENTS

My acknowledgements are due to West Midlands Arts for their award to me of a bursary. My thanks also to Christopher Whelen for his helpful comments; it was he who drew my attention to the last poem. "How Brief the Night" was published in *Corriere della Sera* to commemorate the eightieth anniversary of the poet's birth. It is claimed in the accompanying article as perhaps his last poem, and the date given is August 1967.

Some of these versions were first published in *Selected Poems* (Penguin Modern European Poets, 1965) and in *Debit and Credit*, Quasimodo's last book, published by Anvil Press Poetry in 1972. Individual poems from this collection have appeared in *London Magazine, Stand* and the *Times Literary Supplement*.

Four of the poems were set for voice and instrumental groups by Elizabeth Lutyens in a work entitled *And Suddenly It's Evening*, commissioned by the BBC for the inaugural concerts at the Queen Elizabeth Hall in 1967 and later included in the Promenade Concerts at the Albert Hall.

J. B.

CONTENTS

Introduction | 13
Translator's Note | 23
Prologue: To Salvatore Quasimodo | 25

AND SUDDENLY IT'S EVENING (1920–1942)

WATERS AND LANDS (1920–1929)

And Suddenly It's Evening | 29
Wind at Tindari | 30
Angels | 31
And Your Dress Is White | 32
Tree | 33
Aries | 33
Deadwater | 34
Earth | 34
Day Stoops | 35
Space | 35
Ancient Winter | 36
Sorrow of Things I Do Not Know | 36
There Was a Sound of Airy Seasons Passing | 37
The Dead | 37
No Night So Clear Ever Vanquished You | 38
You Call on a Life | 38
Cool Seashore | 39
Mirror | 39
No One | 40
Alleyway | 41
Greedily I Spread My Hand | 41
Homecomings | 42
Night Birds' Refuge | 43
Even My Company Forsakes Me | 43
Every Form Waylost in Me | 44

SUNKEN OBOE (1930–1932)

Sunken Oboe | 47
The Eucalyptus | 48
To My Land | 49
Birth of Song | 50
Rest of the Grass | 51

In the Ancient Light of the Tides / 52
Word / 53
Young Woman Lying Back in the Midst of the Flowers / 54
Lesser Curve / 55
One Buried in Me Declares / 56
Playmate / 57
Lament of a Friar in an Icon / 58
Without Memory of Death / 59
Prayer to the Rain / 60
Autumn / 61
Mouth of the River Roja / 61
Woods Sleep / 62
To Night / 63
My Patient Day / 63
Metamorphoses in the Saint's Urn / 64
Came Down to Me Through New Innocence / 65
Island / 66
Where the Dead Stand Open-Eyed / 67
Give Me My Day / 68
Convalescence / 69
The Angel / 70
Hidden Life / 71
Changeful with Stars and Quiet / 72
Become Darkness and Height / 73
Water Decomposes Dormice / 74
Seed / 75
First Day / 76
Green Drift / 77
Roads of Rivers in Sleep / 78
Hermaphrodite Earthworm / 79
Suffered Forms of Trees / 80
Living I Sicken / 81
Amen for Sunday in Albis / 82

ERATO AND APOLLYON (1932–1936)

Syllables to Erato / 85
Song of Apollyon / 86
Apollyon / 87
The Ànapo / 88
Dead Heron / 89
On the Hill of the "Terre Bianche" / 90
In Your Light I Am Wrecked / 91
Insomnia / 92

Often a Coastland / 93
Island of Ulysses / 94
Salt-Bed in Winter / 95
Sardinia / 96
In Light of Skies / 97
Quarries / 98
For My Mortal Smell / 98
In the Right Human Time / 99
Alien City / 100
In the Feeling of Death / 101
Of the Sinner of Myths / 102

NEW POEMS (1936–1942)

The Magpie Laughs Black in the Orange Trees / 105
Street in Agrigentum / 106
The Gentle Hill / 107
What Is It, Shepherd of Air? / 108
Before the Statue of Ilaria del Carreto / 109
Now Day Is Breaking / 110
The Rain Is Already With Us / 110
One Evening, Snow / 111
Piazza Fontana / 112
The Tall Sailing Ship / 113
On the Banks of the Lambro / 114
Evening in the Màsino Valley / 116
Elegos for the Dancer Cumani / 118
Delphic Woman / 119
Imitation of Joy / 120
Horses of Moon and Volcanoes / 121
Again a Green River / 122
Beach at St Antiochus / 123
The Meagre Flower Is Already Flying / 124
Threshold of Puberty / 124

DAY AFTER DAY (1943–1946)

On the Willow Boughs / 127
Letter / 128
19 January 1944 / 129
Snow / 130
Day After Day / 130
Perhaps the Heart / 131
Winter Night / 132

Milan, August 1943 / 132
The Wall / 133
O My Gentle Beasts / 134
Written, Perhaps, on a Tomb / 135
This Pilgrim / 136
Fortress of Bergamo Alta / 137
By the Adda / 138
Again I Hear the Sea / 139
Elegy / 139
Of Another Lazarus / 140
The Ferry / 140
Your Silent Foot / 141
Man of My Time / 142

* * *

LIFE IS NOT DREAM (1946–1948)

Lament for the South / 145
Epitaph for Bice Donetti / 146
Dialogue / 147
Colour of Rain and Iron / 148
Almost a Madrigal / 149
Anno Domini MCMXLVII / 150
My Country Is Italy / 151
Thànatos Athànatos / 152
Letter to My Mother / 153

THE FALSE AND TRUE GREEN (1949–1955)

The Dead Guitars / 157
Enemy of Death / 158
The False and True Green / 159
In a Distant City / 160

From Sicily
How Long the Night / 161
Beyond the Waves of the Hills / 161
Near a Saracen Tower, for My Dead Brother / 162
Temple of Zeus at Agrigentum / 163

When the Walls and Trees Fell Down
Laude (29 April 1945) / 164
To the Fifteen of Piazzale Loreto / 165
Auschwitz / 166

10

To the Cervi Brothers, to Their Italy / 168

Epigrams
To a Hostile Poet / 170
From the Web of Gold / 170

THE INCOMPARABLE EARTH (1955–1958)

Visible, Invisible
Visible, Invisible / 173
The Incomparable Earth / 174
Today, the Twenty-First of March / 175
From Disfigured Nature / 176
An Open Arc / 177
A Copper Amphora / 178
To My Father / 179
The Tombs of the Scaligers / 181
An Act or a Name of the Spirit / 182

Still of Hell
The Wall / 183
In This City / 184
Still of Hell / 185
News Item / 186
Almost an Epigram / 187
Soldiers Weep by Night / 188

From Greece
At Night on the Acropolis / 189
Mycenae / 190
Following the Alpheus /191
Delphi / 192
Marathon / 193
Minotaur at Knossos / 193
Eleusis / 194

Questions and Answers
To the New Moon / 195
An Answer / 196
Another Answer / 197

Two Inscriptions
Inscription for the Fallen of Marzabotto / 198
Inscription for the Partisans of Valenza / 199

DEBIT AND CREDIT (1959–1965)

Debit and Credit / 203
Varvàra Alexandrovna / 204
Only If Love Should Pierce You / 205
A September Night / 206
Along the Isar / 207
From the Shores of the Balaton / 208
Tollbridge / 209
The Negro Church at Harlem / 210
Cape Caliakra / 211
The Silence Does Not Deceive Me / 212
Glendalough / 213
Tuscan Crossbowmen / 214
In Chiswick Cemetery / 215
The Maya at Mérida / 216
Words to a Spy / 217
Love Poem / 218
I Have Lost Nothing / 218
On the Island / 219
To Liguria / 221
Imperceptible Time / 222
Enough One Day to Balance the World / 223
I Have Flowers and at Night Call on the Poplars / 224

TWO UNCOLLECTED POEMS

Lines to Angiola Maria / 225
How Brief the Night / 227

DISCOURSE ON POETRY / 229

Epilogue: To Salvatore Quasimodo / 239

Bibliography / 240
Index of Titles / 241
Index of First Lines / 244

INTRODUCTION

Salvatore Quasimodo was born in Sicily at Syracuse in 1901, the son of a station-master. His early days were spent in eastern Sicily, at Roccalimera, Gela, Acquaviva, Trabia and Messina. There, at the time of the earthquake, at the age of seven, he absorbed the images of death and disaster, and witnessed the shooting of thieves "caught in the rubble and executed in the dark / by firing squads from the landing parties." At Palermo he began his studies as an engineer, and in the land of myth, sulphur and salt-mines, of peasant women in black, waters and Greek remains, the recurring themes of his later poetry were born – death, silence and solitude. They recur, as Carlo Bernari* has pointed out, in 84 of his 173 lyric poems. One could add to these the prevailing sense of deprivation and exile, the result of his "rupture" from "the incomparable earth" of the south.

By the end of the First World War, having completed his intermediate studies, he left Sicily to study for an engineering degree at the Rome Polytechnic. Circumstances forced him to suspend his studies and take various jobs in order to live. He was employed as a technical designer, then as a shop assistant in a hardware store. During this period of casual employment, in 1921, he began to study Greek and to read Dante, Petrarch, Tasso, Plato, St Augustine and Spinoza, all strong influences on his later development as a poet. In 1926 he returned to the south as an employee in the Ministry of Public Works at Reggio Calabria, having qualified as a surveyor. There, in company with old friends from Messina, every Sunday for the next three years he read, talked and wrote poetry. These were years of inspired apprenticeship. The group numbered among them Pugliatti, Natoli, Antò, La Pira, Saggio and Patti. The Sunday gatherings included trips to Tindari,

* *Quasimodo between Eros and Thanatos*, Marotta, 1969.

13

and the fine "Wind at Tindari" (p. 30) was the result of one of these. Vittorini, who had married Quasimodo's sister, introduced him to the Solaria, a cultural group based in Florence. It included Loria, Montale, Vittorini and Bonsanti. The latter published his first three poems in the Solaria magazine, and shortly after *Waters and Lands* was published in 1930.

In the next few years he lived at Imperia, near San Remo, where he was involved in building a military road with 1,500 workers, then in Sardinia, and in 1938 he moved to Milan. At this point, after trouble with his administrative superiors, he was forced into a period of exile in Valtellina. He finally gave up his job, abandoned the career he had trained for, and dedicated himself to his literary activities. Another volume of poems was published, and in the following year he joined the staff of *Tempo*. He was offered, and took up, the post of Professor of Italian Literature at the Milan Conservatory of Music in 1940. His *Greek Lyrics* was published, and this gave him national standing in the world of Italian letters. The publication in 1942 of *And Suddenly It's Evening* set the seal on his pre-war opus.

He gained the San Babila Prize in 1950, shared the Etna-Taormina Prize with Dylan Thomas in 1953, and in 1958 he won the Viareggio Prize. In 1959 the award to Quasimodo of the Nobel Prize for Literature for his poetry "wh ch with classical fire expresses the tragic experience of life in our time" indicated that an international audience was at last ready to acknowledge Italian poetic achievement. His poetic creed is outlined in an essay entitled "Discourse on Poetry" which was included in his 1956 collection of poems *The False and True Green*.

The award was greeted with mixed feelings in Italy; delight that it had been given to an Italian poet, and regret that both Ungaretti and Montale, the two "senior" poets of the triumvirate, had been overlooked. The award obviously focused on the post-war poetry, the "committed" poetry which followed the 1942 collection *And Suddenly It's*

Evening. Critics noted a change of voice, and preferred the hermetic verse of the pre-war years. Since his death in 1968, with the whole span of the work before us, the division which seemed to mark off his pre-war and post-war poetry seems illusory. The event of the war experience in Italy certainly produced new urgencies, undeniable pressures, and some of the "committed" poems have the declamatory shrillness of "public" poetry. But a close inspection of the whole output after the war indicates an absorption of that galvanic experience into the modes and themes which again characterize the poet at his best; a highly individual voice, and a personal experience universalized. It would be wrong to misunderstand the controversy and infer from it that Quasimodo has had less than his share of critical acclaim among Italian critics, though the poet himself, in the nine years following the award until his death in 1968, complained of neglect by his compatriots, and a sense of isolation. Annamaria Angioletti, his young mistress during the last eight years of his life, writes of the ceremony in June 1967 at Oxford University when Harold Macmillan, then Chancellor, presented the poet with an honorary degree:

"In June 1967, a year before his death, Salvatore Quasimodo had another moment of happiness after the Nobel. Yet again it was a foreign country which accorded him the tribute of recognition by men undivided by parochial faction or, worse, favouritism; men who accepted the international judgement, at peace with nature, science and God; men like Leonardo. His own country until the time of his death, and even on that occasion, showed him hostility, envy or malice."

But the long list of poets and critics who have written about him, among them Solmi, Macri, Montale, Bo, Florae, Anceschi, Robertis, Contini, Antonielli, is testimony to the fact that his poetry has had due examination and recognition among his countrymen.

The distinction, then, between the earlier and later climate of his poetry should not be exaggerated. The poet's own critical statements may, ironically, have falsified the perspectives through which his later poetry was viewed. He speaks of the growth of a "social poetry" which aspires to "dialogue rather than monologue", towards the dramatic and epic rather than the gnomic. "Today, after two wars... he [the poet] must re-make man." The poet's own phrases suggest that he aimed at moving from a position of withdrawal to one of participation; admirable aims, socio-politically orientated to a post-war age. But their terms are misleading, and emphasize a distinction which does not exist between the best of his earlier and later poetry. When I was invited to translate Quasimodo, and he suggested that we should meet, I declined the invitation precisely on these grounds; that I might be tempted to translate his intentions instead of his poems.

Between 1930 and 1938 Quasimodo was one of a number of poets whose poetry was described as "hermetic". The Hermetic school, as it became known, had its roots among the French symbolists. It was a poetry of verbal ambivalence, achieving a direct impact by its emotive use of language. It aimed at evoking rather than describing, and avoided the merely decorative. This was *poesia pura,* image evoking object. With the war (Quasimodo insists that war changes the vital life of a people) his poetry became one of dedication to the moral experience of wartime Italy, and some of the poems show a change of tone and texture. His theme is the plight of man, his history, his fate in a disruptive universe. He measures his present against his past, probes his conscience. The poems are full of interrogatives. They speak of innocence, loss of innocence, animals and vegetation, the cosmos. They convey pride and shame, a sense of lost worlds, defeat, exile and violence. They represent a search for meaning at a time when meaning seemed to have vanished. In spite of their directness, the poems are sometimes obscure, enigmatic, complex. There is a power behind then which dissolves the surface incongruities and reveals a universe which remains unviolated.

16

One must surrender to these poems on their own terms. They are profound, but without cleverness, subtle without artifice. Though they derive from a highly personal experience, they achieve larger meanings. Even the sparse, explicit reporting of "News Item" (p. 186) does this. There is, throughout, the same unifying experience behind the austerity and passion. He is no product of a poetic movement, has absorbed influences but remained intact, firm in his own nature and form. The changes in his poetics, from the first books, are true reflections of his metabolism as a poet. The line of Italian poetry which leads in the nineteenth century through Carducci and Pascoli to D'Annunzio, seemed to look forward to a kind of poet *par excellence* who would fulfil the tradition of eloquence and bring it to maturity. The reticence, the refusal of this invitation offered by the past, is at the root of Quasimodo's achievement on the ground prepared by Ungaretti. One is reminded of a similar break with tradition in England after the First World War. Like Ungaretti and Montale, Quasimodo absorbed French influences and evolved a language appropriate to his purposes, tuned to the exploration of new inner dimensions. It enables him to look directly both at and through his objects, to pursue his remoter searches and to identify his experience with strange ease. Objects become images without losing their identity, and speak with their own voices. Their latent power is released, so that they participate in the organization of language, giving word and word-pattern a resonance which is not mere eloquence. Quasimodo has outgrown classifications such as "Hermetic" or "Resistance". In the war he wrote of human dignity, mortal aspiration, man's inhumanity, both as general themes and as closely felt personal experiences. The ambivalence never becomes poetic obscurantism, and the poems make their demands on the whole personality, the heart-mind. Always the poems prevail, entire, as poems, and rarely subside into unresolved para-poems. His special capacity is to organize a complex, many-dimensioned experience into a poetry which

17

renders that experience directly without losing any of its complexity or impetus.

The disunity of Italian history, and the nature of the language with its cadences, harmonies, arpeggios and pizzicatos may account for the rarity of this in Italian poetry. After Petrarch there is no John Donne. There are barriers beyond which poets did not reach out to their experience. It may be for similar reasons that Italy, so great an influence on the development of English drama in the Renaissance, produced no body of notable drama. It is as if the harmonies so abundant in the language predisposed its poets to manipulate rather than exploit it. So often the record has been of indulgence rather than abstinence. The signal achievement of Quasimodo and his two fellow poets seems to be not so much their renewal of language as the development of a new attitude to it, a wiser reticence. Quasimodo is concerned with speech, not song, organization, not symmetry.

Oracle, prayer, myth, Eden, exile, childhood, death, solitude, against a background of skies, lands, waters and people; these are his themes. The general becomes personal. A name of honour becomes a personal love, a personal love becomes an archetypal image. Dante, Donne and Blake achieve this kind of "through-shine" poetic transmutation. His incongruities, almost quaintnesses, indicate a freedom from his own technical accomplishment. He never betrays his experience by avoiding them. He is wary of the Italian heritage of eloquence from Petrarch down to the "Crepuscular" and Futurist poetry of his own day that "can not distinguish poetry from literature". For Quasimodo poetry is man. The poet "modifies the world with his liberty and truth." But we must turn to his poetry, not to his theories, to find his particular brand of truth, or we may find ourselves recalling Shelley's *Defence of Poetry* and its passionate legislations. When he speaks of poetry since 1945 as dealing with "the real world, with common words" we are inclined to recall Wordsworth's Preface to *Lyrical*

Ballads, with its "language really used by men" and "incidents and situations from common life", and to feel that theories about art are generally *post facto* justifications rather than prescriptions, and that we have heard them all before. "Experience" in Quasimodo's best poems seems to be archetypal, anthropological, geological, vegetal as well as social and personal... a vast intergrowth reflected from the poet's "underground", where all the meeting streams with their sub-aqueous growths are catalysed. In this context of archetypal modes, the purely social or political was a passing guest, who shouted a word or two in a time of agony for man and left, leaving the sub-terrestrial, the aquatic, the voices of the air to speak, and continue their dialogue from the beyond. Quasimodo, a *siculo greco,* tuned finely by his translations from the poetry of several languages, imbued with a strong sense of race history and immanent being, may be best approached, for all his "poet of the common man" acclaim, as an oracle or a medium.

In writing of Quasimodo, however briefly, it is difficult to "place" him in focus without reference to his two senior contemporaries, Ungaretti and Montale. All three had absorbed the Italian poetic tradition down to Carducci, Pascoli and D'Annunzio, and had found ways not unlike those Eliot found of breaking from "a worn-out poetical fashion", or of modifying it for what they had to say as men of their time. Like Eliot they had all drunk deep at the fountain of French symbolism. Ungaretti and Montale were both, from the start, literary men, in regular contact with poets and the cultural milieu. Ungaretti's first poems were in French (he lived in Paris for several years) and at the Sorbonne he had an academic training and made the acquaintance of many of the notable artists and writers at the turn of the century. He was never an outsider to the literary scene. Montale started his career as a literary critic and journalist. He led the life of an academic, a scholar and poet. In this they differed from Quasimodo, the Sicilian, the poor boy "who ran away at night / in a skimpy coat with a few

19

lines / of poetry in his pocket", started his training as an engineer, and was employed by the Ministry of Public Works while he sweated out his literary education in his own time. Montale and Quasimodo expressed the conscience of their time, the former with uncompromising pessimism and gloom, the latter with more passion and compassion. Ungaretti's contribution was mainly a stylistic one, a focus on the word and on stripping language down to its essentials. In this he led the way for the other two poets, with the French symbolists a constant presence. All three perfected their art by translating. The sense of myth, the search for Eden is strong in Ungaretti and Quasimodo. In Montale's poetry there is no such impulse, only an offered wasteland, an unrelieved moon landscape with man isolated in the "stony rubbish", his sole conviction that "hell is certain". In Quasimodo's poem "Thànatos Athànatos" (p. 152) the dialogue of despair alters.

> ... There
> beyond the smoke of mist, within the trees
> the power of the leaves keeps watch,
> the river, pressing its banks, is true.
> Life is not dream. Man with his jealous
> lament of silence is true. ...

Ungaretti's tone is calm, resigned and disciplined in the face of war and human misery. Montale writes of things as empty symbols of man's situation. Quasimodo protests. The objects he sees are infused with life, the supra-human vitality of nature from which he is always seeking to draw "influence" (the neo-platonic term seems apt). He aspires, longs, hopes, while Montale is resigned. All three poets refined the language of poetry by stripping it of "eloquence" and ornament. Ungaretti, with stylistic concerns in mind, stripped it down to its essentials ("M'illumino/d'immenso"). Montale made it a suitable vehicle for the nightmare emptiness of his vision, and Quasimodo ordered it as a means of conveying images of death, solitude and love in a

20

universe full of latent power and meaning. Significantly, it is only in poems such as the "Two Inscriptions" (pp. 198–9) that Quasimodo's language of overt commitment relapses into good rhetoric, the pressurized speech of mere "protest".

Debit and Credit ("Dare e avere") contains his last poems, written between 1959 and 1965, his last years of illness and travel. It was published in 1966 and followed *Collected Poems,* published in 1960. The title echoes the final line of the poem "News Item" in that volume. The poems are mostly place poems. "The blood of the wars has dried", he says in the opening poem, the hour of pity has gone, but:

> In my voice
> there is at least a sign
> of living geometry.

This "living geometry" measures places and times. It traces the same questions as the pre-war poetry, is less "hermetic", but not dominated by the aim of "re-making man". The poems provide a development, and in many ways a culmination, to the mainstream of his poetry, and are rich in dimensions which some of the war poems lack. There is a wider range of places, with different but similar landmarks and there are recurring confrontations with death, the past, life. Serious illness in distant places brings him to a more intimate dialogue with death. "Perhaps I am always dying", he says, as he listens to

> the words of life
> I have never understood.

It is a poetry of the antecamera of death, or life, and in this half beyond, a kind of no-man's-land, he explores carefully

> the absurd
> difference that runs
> between death and the illusion
> of the heart's beating.

21

He may now write from a Moscow hospital, a negro church in Harlem, a cemetery at Chiswick, or from Mérida in Mexico, but he meets the same ghosts as he did at Agrigentum or on the Naviglio in Milan. Now he knows them better and can meet them more intimately. There is a note of acceptance that he has not penetrated the mystery, and of faith in a present that shapes another present. Because of love he can trace a possible link between life and death, and he glad that "visible time begins again" in the moment of reprieve.

These last poems seem to have a rightful place at the summit of Quasimodo's achievement. We are not likely to turn to them in the same spirit as to "Wind at Tindari" (p. 30) or "Ancient Winter" (p. 36). Nor are we likely to quote them from platforms, or read them in public at poetry festivals. The Polish poet Miłosz asks: "What is poetry which does not save / nations or people? / A connivance with official lies, / a song of drunkards whose throats will be cut in a moment, / readings for sophomore girls." The division is false. Quasimodo's own phrase "to re-make man" is a more accurate touchstone to his poetry than this, which is a cry more in keeping with his wartime poetry, and I quote it as an instance of the kind of commitment from which he progressed. In *Debit and Credit* he has voyaged beyond public speech to a "dialogue with the beyond". The poems are meditations, rehearsals of the conflict between being and non-being. The dead of Glendalough, Foscolian echoes in Chiswick Cemetery, the living-dead Maya at Mérida in Mexico mingle their voices with the sound of his own name, pre-heard as it is suddenly spoken over the loudspeakers after his death, at Balatonfüred in Hungary, "like a warning of rain squalls".

If we do not read them in the days of our protest or anger, we shall certainly turn to them when the visible becomes invisible, and we are ready to listen more willingly to the words of life we have never understood.

JACK BEVAN

TRANSLATOR'S NOTE

Some poetry transcends language. What we recognize in some parts of Wordsworth is the experience which is not merely a literary experience. Quasimodo's poetry, though he is a master in a literary sense, lies beyond the constrictions of a particular language. He may be less susceptible to the ills of translation than some other poets, and more capable of continuing to transmit, in another language, on almost the same frequency. This is not to preclude from his poetry in Italian its fullest rights. We recognize Dante as a greater poet than Petrarch for just these reasons.

When Quasimodo has been translated, we are faced with the same kind of problem as his readers in Italian; the problem of the poetry, of coming to grips with the experience, of seeing images in objects, and objects in images. The main focus appears not to be that of language-image-object, but of object-image-object. Or, to put it another way, the tensions between object and image are more significant than those between language and image, or language and object. So that resolving him is not mainly the translator's problem; it is the reader's.

At the time when I was first asked by Penguin Books to translate a selection of Quasimodo's poems he was only a name to me, and I was virtually unacquainted with his work. I must say that after the first shock of delight at my first sip I drank deep at his well. When young I had fed on Catullus and the European poets who handled the theme of mutability through the Middle Ages and Renaissance down to the nineteenth century and beyond. In them all I could trace a family voice which changed only in timbre with the generations. Eliot and the poets of the thirties, though innovators in some ways, had marked features of their lineage. Only Donne and Hopkins among English poets seemed to be true mavericks, and I recall a similar shock on first reading their poetry. Yet Quasimodo is not in any profound sense an innovator. He helped to modify the language of poetry, as did his two fellow poets, Ungaretti and Montale, as Eliot, Wordsworth and Dante did. But his uniqueness lies elsewhere. Those who read these translations may agree that he is a different kind of poet from any they have read before, or merely that he evokes responses which are different. In either case, what is striking is that throughout these highly individual poems there runs a unity that binds them together as a collection.

The enigmatic "you" is ever present, sometimes an unseen presence, sometimes himself, or someone from the past, or the person to whom the poem is addressed. These presences fuse together, keep us on our toes, and sharpen our response, so that we read with all our senses alert. Not to do so leads us wildly astray. Strange irradiations run through the fabric. Sometimes dead ones speak, or river gods rise with vegetal growths on them. We see dormice from funeral windows in the "vegetal dark" and enter the poet's dream as if it were our own. Suddenly we are back in his childhood, the dead young woman laid out, and we smell the flowers. Or we hear sounds in the dark, and waken to mysterious modes of our own being. We hear from its bush the last cicada of summer with the siren "deep wailing" its warning over the plain of Lombardy, hear in the winter night the village tower dripping dark, see "dead Solunto" down there among the hare's lentisks. We wake with him in a Chirico streetscape and "follow silent houses where the dead stand open-eyed", and realize that we, too, "shall have voices of the dead". Such images cohere in poems which echo in the memory.

As translator I have tried to preserve this echo as accurately and as disturbingly as it was transmitted. Ambiguities remain as in the originals. The various addressees remain as "you". Abruptnesses and quaintnesses, disconcerting tense changes, weightings and syntactical emphases I have tried to keep intact, so that the poetry can be more accurately *overheard*.*

J. B.

* "Eloquence is *heard*, poetry is *overheard*" – J. S. Mill

PROLOGUE: TO SALVATORE QUASIMODO

Grouted from lands of marsh and fire
and giant myth where you sucked
the lava still in your veins;
plucked from your orange-groves, the harsh
hermetic fruit like blood on your limbs
spattered by war,
you have taken a graft
and grown a poplar of the northern plains,
telegraph wires in your leaves, your roots
reaching all down the map towards Arethusa.

Ancient telamon risen up from the dead
of your race, speak
through my mouth, breathe your life in my breath;
and if my own voice speaks, hurl your
gigantic boulders after me into the sea.

JACK BEVAN

AND SUDDENLY IT'S EVENING

Waters and Lands
1920–1929

AND SUDDENLY IT'S EVENING

Each of us is alone on the heart of the earth
pierced by a ray of sun:
and suddenly it's evening.

WIND AT TINDARI

Tindari, I know you gentle
in broad hills hung over waters
of the god's sweet isles;
today you assail me
and lean into my heart.

I climb peaks, airy steeps
wound in the pine winds,
and the happy crew that goes with me
fades in the air,
a wave of sounds and love:
and you take me,
you from whom I drew evil,
and fear of shades and silence, –
once sure retreats of sweetness –
and death of spirit.

To you the earth is unknown
where each day I sink
and nourish secret words;
other light unleafs you on the windows
in your nocturnal dress,
and joy not mine
rests on your breast.

Exile is bitter
and my search for peace
that ended with you, changes today
to an early wishing for death;
and every love is a screen from sadness.
mute step into the dark
where you have placed
bitter bread for me to break.

Tindari, return serene;
rouse me, mild friend
to thrust me to the sky from a rock,
pretending fear to those who do not
know what deep wind has sought me out.

ANGELS

Lost to you all sweetness in life,
you cherish dreams; let the unknown shore
come before day to meet you
where calm waters move slowly on
crowded with angels of green circling trees.

Let it be infinite, crown your every hour
in time that seems eternal,
youth's smile, the pain,
where in secret you sought
the birth of day and night.

AND YOUR DRESS IS WHITE

You have bent your head, are looking at me;
and your dress is white,
and a breast blooms from the loosed
lace on your left shoulder.

The light exceeds me; trembles
and falls on your naked arms.

Again I see you. Your words
were quick, tight-spoken,
giving me heart
in the weight of a circus-like
life I knew.

The road was deep
that the wind went down
certain March nights,
and woke us unknown
like the first time.

TREE

From you a shadow melts
making mine seem dead,
though with its motion it quivers
or breaks fresh sky-blue water
by the banks of the Ànapo where I return
this evening impelled by lunar March,
rich already with grasses and wings.

I live not by shadow alone;
earth and sun, and the sweet gift of water
have renewed your every leaf,
while I go bowed and dry,
and touch your bark with my face.

ARIES

In the lazy moving of skies
the season shows itself: a sign to the wind,
to the almond tree, to clear
plains of shade, airy
clouds of shadows and wheat:
re-unites the buried
voices of riverbeds and ditches
and the fabulous days of grace.

Each green thing opens.
And a brooding of icy laurels,
bare, pagan gods, wraps the sequestered waters;
look, they rise up from the gravel on the bottom,
upside down in celestial sleep.

DEADWATER

Closed water, sleep of the marshes
broad-streaked, soaking poison,
now white, now green in lightning flashes,
you are like my heart.

Around, the grey of poplar and ilex,
leaves and acorns still within,
each with its uni-centred circles
frayed by the dark southwester drone.

So as on water memory
spreads its widening rings, my heart
moves from one point out and dies,
sister to you, deadwater.

EARTH

Night, serene shades,
cradle of air,
if I spread myself in you the wind arrives
with sea smell of the earth
where my countrymen sing on the shore
to sails, and nets,
and children awake before dawn.

Dry hills, plains of first grass
awaiting herdsmen and floods,
your disease is inside me, scooping me out.

DAY STOOPS

You find me forsaken, Lord,
in your day,
locked from all light.

Without you I go in dread,
lost road of love,
and have no grace,
fearful even to confess,
so my wishes are barren.

I have loved you, fought you;
day stoops
and I gather shades from the skies;
how sad my heart
of flesh.

SPACE

I am closed in a dark
circle's centre,
escape useless.
Sometimes a child, not mine,
sings there; short is the space and it
smiles on dead angels.

It breaks me: and is love on earth,
that is good even though its chasms
of waters, of stars, of light,
boom; even though it waits, deserted paradise,
for its god of soul and of stone.

ANCIENT WINTER

Desire of your bright
hands in the flame's half-light;
flavour of oak, roses
and death.

Ancient winter.

The birds seeking the grain
were suddenly snow.

So words:
a little sun; a haloed glory,
then mist; and the trees
and us, air, in the morning.

SORROW OF THINGS I DO NOT KNOW

A tangle of black and white roots
smelling of ferment and worms,
cut by the waters – earth.

Sorrow of things I do not know
is born in me: another death
always to feel on my heart weigh
with the grass, a sod.

THERE WAS A SOUND OF AIRY SEASONS PASSING

A wry smile cut your face,
gave me deep hurt;
an echo of full agonies
revived as I touched dim
signs of joy on the flesh.

There was a sound of airy seasons passing,
bareness of mornings,
unsteady beams colliding.

Another sun, from which this
weight of silent soliloquy came.

THE DEAD

It seemed as if voices were raised,
lips sought waters,
hands were raised to skies.

What skies! Whiter than the dead
that always waken me gently;
barefoot, they do not go far away.

Gazelles were drinking at the springs;
wind stirring junipers,
and branches lifting the stars?

NO NIGHT SO CLEAR EVER VANQUISHED YOU

No night so clear ever vanquished you
if you open yourself up to laughter and all seems to touch
a stairway of stars
that once in dream came spiralling down,
putting me back in time.

Then God was fear of a closed room
where a dead one lies,
centre of all things,
clear sky and wind, ocean and cloud.

And my throwing myself on the ground,
my crying the name out loud in the silence
was sweetness of feeling myself alive.

YOU CALL ON A LIFE

Languor of love, sadness;
you call on a life
that inside, deep, has names
of skies and gardens.

And would it were my flesh
that transforms the gift of evil.

COOL SEASHORE

I compare my man's life to you,
cool seashore, drawing pebbles and light
and forgetting with the new wave
the one that once the air's moving gave voice to.

If you rouse me I listen,
and every pause is sky I lose myself in,
calm of trees and the night's transparency.

MIRROR

Look! on the trunk
buds break:
a newer green than the grass,
balm to the heart:
the trunk seemed already dead,
leaning over the gully.

And everything seems to me like a miracle;
I am that water of clouds
reflecting so blue today
its piece of sky in the ditches,
this green, bursting the bark,
that even last night was not there.

NO ONE

I am perhaps a child
afraid of the dead,
but whom death calls
in order to free him from all living things:
children, trees, insects;
from all things having the heart of sadness:

because he has no more gifts
and the roads are dark,
and there is no one any more
who can make him weep
next to you, Lord.

ALLEYWAY

Sometimes your voices call me back,
and what skies and waters
waken inside me!

A net of sunlight tears
on your walls that at night
were a swaying of lamps
from the late shops
full of wind and sadness.

Other times: a loom thumped in the courtyard,
and at night could be heard a whimper
of puppies and babies.

Alley: a cross of houses
calling out low to each other,
never knowing it is the fear
of being alone in the dark.

GREEDILY I SPREAD MY HAND

In poverty of flesh I am here,
Father, as I am; road dust
that the wind scarce raises in pardon.

But although time was when I could not rend
my voice still artless and raw,
greedily I spread my hand:
give me suffering, daily food.

41

HOMECOMINGS

Piazza Navona, in the dark I lay
full length on the seats in search of rest,
and my eyes with lines and spirals
joined up the stars,
the ones I followed as a child
stretched on the pebbles of the Platani,
spelling my prayers to the dark.

Hands clasped under my head
I recalled the times I returned,
the smell of fruit drying on hurdles,
of wallflowers, lavender, ginger;
when I thought of softly reading to you
(you and I, mother, in a corner of shade)
the tale of the Prodigal Son
that always followed in the silences
like a rhythm extending at every step
beyond my will.

But for the dead there is no returning
and no time, not even for a mother
when the road calls;
and I left once more, enclosed in night
as if afraid to remain at dawn.

And the road gave me the songs
that savour of swelling ears of corn,
the flower that whites the olive groves
in among jonquils and blue of flax;
echoes in eddies of dust,
chants of men and creaking carts,
their meagre, flickering lanterns
no more than a firefly's light.

NIGHT BIRDS' REFUGE

High up stands a twisted pine;
intent, it listens over the chasm,
its trunk bent like a bow.

Refuge of nightbirds,
in the deepest hour it resounds
with swift wings' beating.

My heart, too, has a nest
hung in the dark, a voice;
it, too, listens in the night.

EVEN MY COMPANY FORSAKES ME

Even my company forsakes me,
the ghetto women, jokers of the taverns
with whom I spent most time,
and the girl is dead
whose face was always aglow
with the oil of unleavened dough
and her dark, Jewish flesh.

Even my sadness perhaps
has changed, as if I were not my own,
forgotten, even by me.

EVERY FORM WAYLOST IN ME

Other life held me: alone
among people unknown; few gifts of bread.
Every form waylost in me,
love, beauty, from which the child drew
delusion, and sadness after.

Sunken Oboe

1930–1932

SUNKEN OBOE

Delay your favour, grasping pain,
in this my hour
of desired abandon.

An oboe coldly syllables
delight of timeless leaves,
not mine, and forgets;

in me evening is falling;
it is waterset
on my grassy hands.

Wings flit in a limp sky
trembling; the heart migrates,
leaving me fallow,

and my days, rubble.

THE EUCALYPTUS

No sweetness ripens me,
and painfully time
drifts day by day
reviving with breath
of harsh resins.

A tree wavers in me
from a sleepy shore,
winged air
breathes out bitter leaves.

You pierce me, grieving re-greening,
childhood smell
that coveted joy welcomed,
sick then from a secret love
of reciting to waters.

Island of the morning:
at half-light re-rises
the golden fox
that was killed at a mountain spring.

TO MY LAND

A sun breaks swollen in sleep
and trees howl;
adventurous dawn
where you steer unanchored
and the mild coastal seasons
ferment shores into birth.

Here I awaken, sick,
bitter with another land
and the changeable mercy of song
that love of men and death
germinates in me.

My ills show new green
but my hands are air
to your branches,
to women whom sadness
closed up in despair,
whom time that greys me, strips
my bark, never touches.

I throw myself into you: cool
of aisles comes to rest in my heart:
naked footsteps of angels
are heard there in the dark.

BIRTH OF SONG

Water-spring: light reappearing:
leaves burn rosy.

Ice on brimming rivers
where islands are,
mirrors of shadows and stars.

And your bosom of blue confounds me,
never feeding
with delight my other life.

I die to have you again,
even deluded,
youth, with your feeble
limbs.

REST OF THE GRASS

Drift of light: changing whirlpools,
airy zones of suns,
rising steeps: I break the clod
that is mine, stretch myself out. And sleep:
through ages the grass has been resting
its heart with me.

Death wakes me:
more one, more alone,
deep beating of the wind:
of night.

IN THE ANCIENT LIGHT OF THE TIDES

Island city
sunk in my heart,
now I go down in the ancient light
of the tides, by tombs
on the edge of waters
loosed by delight
of dreamed trees.

I call to myself: amorous echo
reflects a sound,
and its secret is sweet, rebounding
in spreading avalanches of air.

A weariness
of unripe rebirths
languishes in me,
the wonted penance of being mine
in an hour beyond time.

And I hear your dead
in the jealous pulsing
of vegetal veins
shallower lying:

an intent breathing of nostrils.

WORD

You laugh at me, flaying myself for words,
bending around me the straining elms,
the blue hedge of skies and hills
and quivering waters' voices,
wiling my youth
with clouds and hues
the light submerges.

I know you. Waylost in you
beauty lifts your breasts,
scoops to your hips and in gentle sweep
spreads over your shy sex,
flows down in harmony of forms
to the ten shells of your lovely feet.

But wait; if I take you,
you too become word to me, and sadness.

YOUNG WOMAN LYING BACK
IN THE MIDST OF THE FLOWERS

One could sense the secret season
in the boding of night rains,
in the sky's varying waves
of light cradle clouds;
I was dead.

A city suspended in air
my last banishment,
and gentle women of long
ago calling around me;
my mother, made new by the years,
sweet hand choosing the whitest
roses to bind my head.

It was night outside,
the stars following their fixed
unknown ways in arcs of gold,
and fleeting things
drew me in secret places
telling of gardens open wide,
and the sense of life;
but for me, grief for the last smile

of a young woman lying back in the midst of the flowers.

LESSER CURVE

Lose me, Lord, that I may not hear
the sunken, silent years denude me,
change the penance to open motion:
the lesser curve
of life is left me.

Make me wind that sails in gladness,
or barley seed, or leper seed
that tells itself in full becoming.
And let loving you be easy
in grass that shoots to the light,
in the sore that holes the flesh.

I attempt a life:
all go barefoot and waver
in search.

Again you leave me: alone I am
in the shadow that stretches to evening,
and no channel opens
to the gentle outflowing of the blood.

ONE BURIED IN ME DECLARES

I banish myself; shadow
of myrtles brims over
and the drowsed space stretches me out.

And love brings no happy
woodland concord closer
in the lone hour with me:
paradise and marsh
sleep in the hearts of the dead.

And one buried in me declares
that the stone-quarry strains
like a root, and probes signs
of the opposite road.

PLAYMATE

I do not know what light you gave me:
the wedded ellipse of blue and white
plunges, landslides inside me. You are come,
blessed birth, to touch me, evoking in silence
the shapes of childhood:
those mild eyes of the stabbed sheep,
my dog whom they killed,
rough, shabby playmate
with bony shoulder-blades.

That boy I loved
more than the others: nimble
at tip-and-run and quoits,
and always silent, without a smile.

We grew in sight of high skies,
voyaging lands and vaporous planets;
mysterious trips by lantern light;
and sleep at last enclosed me lapped
in the peaceful songs of the chicken roost
at the first clog-clatter near the ovens
of the half-dressed servant girls.

You have given me pain,
and the light will not reveal your name,
only that lamb-white name
of the heart that I have buried away.

LAMENT OF A FRIAR IN AN ICON

I live in great drought,
my God;
my green squalor!

Night is buzzing loud,
on fire with insects;

the girdle unfastens
my rotted woollen habit:

I card my flesh
gnawed by roundworms:
love, my skeleton.

Hidden, deep, a corpse
chews earth sodden with urine:

I repent
of having given you my blood,
Lord, my refuge:

have mercy!

WITHOUT MEMORY OF DEATH

Spring raises trees and rivers;
I do not hear the deep voice,
beloved, lost in you.

Without memory of death,
joined in the flesh,
the rumble of final day
wakens us, adolescents.

No one listens to us;
the light breathing of the blood!

My hand
made a branch
flowers on your side.

From plants, stones, waters,
the animals are born
to the blowing of the air.

PRAYER TO THE RAIN

Tang of the sky
on green things;
early evening rain.

Naked voice I listen to you:
and the ploughed heart
takes sweet first fruits of sound and refuge from you;
and you cheer me, mute adolescent,
surprised by other life and every motion
of resurrections undergone
that the dark expresses and transforms.

Holiness of the heavenly time,
of its light
of hanging waters;

of our heart,
of veins open
upon the earth.

AUTUMN

Mild autumn, I possess myself
and bend to your waters to drink the sky,
soft flight of trees and chasms.

Harsh pain of birth
finds me conjoined with you;
and in you I burst and am healed:

poor fallen thing
that earth gathers up.

MOUTH OF THE RIVER ROJA

The deep brasses of the wind
deaden my song
and with limbs parted you endure
the inhuman voice.

Youth, severed from me,
autumns with its last
stirrings, and declines.

Evening is here, the last to come,
a torment of albatrosses;
there are bitter pools in the estuary
sand, contagion with desolate waters.

Doomed exile,
raise up my life of the fallen.

WOODS SLEEP

Dry womb of love and young,
for long years I have wept
beside you, derelict.

Woods of green
and wind sleep serene,
plains where sulphur
was the summer of myths,
motionless.

You had not come to live in me,
omen of endless pain to be:
the land died on the waters,
ancient hands gathered
papyrus in the rivers.

I cannot hate you: so
light my hurricane heart.

TO NIGHT

From your womb
I rise unmindful
and weep.

Angels, silent, walk
with me; things have no breath;
every voice changed into stone,
silence of buried skies.

Your first man
does not know, but grieves.

MY PATIENT DAY

My patient day,
Lord, I bequeath you,
my sickness unhealed,
knees cracked with weariness.

I resign, resign myself;
spring's howl
is a forest
born in my eyes of earth.

METAMORPHOSES IN THE SAINT'S URN

The dead mellow,
my heart with them.
Earth has
mercy for itself in its last mood.

A light from trees of the lake
moves in the glass of the urn:
dark mutation ravages me,
unknown saint: in the scattered seed
green maggots moan:
my face is their springtime.

A memory of dark
at the bottom of walled wells is born,
an echo of buried drums.

I am your worn
relic.

CAME DOWN TO ME THROUGH NEW INNOCENCE

Tonight your voice came down to me
through new innocence, blissful,
and I suffer birth
of broken-hearted joys.

You trembled white,
arms upraised;
and I lay in you
with my life
gathered in a little blood,
forgetting the chant
that made me feel so keenly,
with the woman who plucked me away,

my stunted
tree sadness.

ISLAND

I have only you,
heart of my race

Love of you, my land,
makes me sad when evening looses
dark smells of orange trees,
oleanders, and the torrent
runs on serene with roses
to its mouth, a sheet of silk.

But if I return to your shores
and a sweet voice singingly calls
timorous from the road,
childhood or love, I do not know,
or longing for other skies turns me,
and I hide in lost things.

66

WHERE THE DEAD STAND OPEN-EYED

We shall follow silent houses
where the dead stand open-eyed
and children grown already
in the laugh that saddens them,
and branches beat on silent windows
in the middle of the night.

We too shall have voices of the dead
if ever we really were alive
or the heart of the woods and the mountain
that drove us down to the rivers
wished us no more than dreams.

GIVE ME MY DAY

Give me my day;
that I may seek again
a calm face of years
that a hollow of waters
can restore to transparency;
so I may grieve for the love of myself.

I walk on your heart,
and stars are meeting
in sleepless archipelagos,
night, like brothers to me,

fossil emerged from a tired wave;
a bending of secret orbits
where we are thrust
with the rocks and grasses.

CONVALESCENCE

I feel another death unknown to me
become love, but more than this slow one
that often pushes me to its forms.

Leavings of seaweed:
I search for myself in the dark harmonies
of deep awakenings
on dense shores of sky.

The docile wind
infuses itself in my blood,
and already is voice and shipwreck,
hands that are being reborn:

hands entwined or palm pressing to palm
spreading in resignation.

The dry, grieving heart
is in awe of you,
unpossessed childhood.

THE ANGEL

The angel sleeps
on roses of air,
white, on her side,
lovely hands crossed
in the shade of her lap

My voice wakes her,
she smiles on me;
sprinkled with pollen
her resting cheek.

She sings; my heart besets me,
dim sky of dawn.
The angel is mine;
I possess her: cold.

HIDDEN LIFE

Space and the hour strain on
and portent holds no light
in the grasses' abandon;
and the wind, the fresh wind blows
no skeins of sounds and unexpected splendours,
and when it lulls the sky, too, is alone.

Give me hidden life,
and if you cannot, then hide me away,
airy sea of night.

I wreck: and you hear me in every syllable
that bores its hole out of the earth
and spreads in the shadow,
and grows into tree, or rock, or blood
in anxious life-form
that dies in itself,
myself stripped bare with the anguish
that brings me calm, deepness of love.

CHANGEFUL WITH STARS AND QUIET

And if delight in me overwhelms you,
it is tangle of shadows.
Nothing now
consoles but silence: the changing face
of air and hills brings no fulfilling,
though light rotates its hollow skies
to the bounds of dark.

Changeful with stars and quiet
night casts us out into the swift deceiving:
stones that at every estuary the water erodes.

Children still sleep in your sleep;
but I sometimes heard a howl
break and become flesh;
and beating of hands and a voice
throw open for me sweet unknown things.

BECOME DARKNESS AND HEIGHT

You come into my voice:
and I see the calm light
descend in shadow with beams
making a star cloud round your head.
And me uncertain, marvelling at the angels,
the dead, the air lit up in an arc.

Not mine; but emerged again
in space, you tremble in me,
become darkness and height.

WATER DECOMPOSES DORMICE

Clear dawn of funeral window-panes;
water decomposes dormice
in the vegetal dark,
from the humps of the beeches
filtering insapient
in the hollow trunks.

Time, like the dormice, vanishes:
and the last splash scalds,
ravages with sweetness.

I can find no shelter in you,
abandoned in sleep
after fresh joy:
vainly my blood renews after love.

SEED

Trees of shadows,
islands wrecking in vast aquaria,
weak night
on the earth that is being born:

a sound of wings
of cloud that opens
on my heart:

not a thing dies
that does not live in me.

You see me: so light I am made,
so inward in things
that I walk with the heavens;

that when You will it
you might cast me to seed
already tired of the weight that sleeps.

FIRST DAY

Peace of spreading waters
wakens me in the heart
of ancient hurricanes,
small troubled monster.

The stars in my dark
that crumbled with me
into barren, polarized globes,
between furrows of swift dawns are weightless:
love of rocks and clouds.

My blood, Lord,
is yours: let us die.

GREEN DRIFT

Evening: sorrowing light,
indolent bells founder.
Say no words to me: love of sounds
is silent in me, and the hour is mine
as in the time of communings
with the air and the woods.

Drowsiness came from the skies
down into lunar waters,
houses slept their mountain sleep,
or snow held angels on the alder trees,
and stars on the window-panes,
glazed like paper kites.

Green drift of islands,
landfalls of sailing ships,
the crew that followed seas and clouds
to the chant of oars and rigging
left me their prey:
so naked and white, that to touch her
the voices of rivers and rocks
sounded in secret.

Then the lands rested
on marine deeps,
and fretful stress and life of other motions
happened in engulfed firmaments.

To possess you is awe
all the weeping fulfils,
softness recalling the islands.

ROADS OF RIVERS IN SLEEP

I find you in the happy landing-places,
warmth, almost, of a new joy,
consort of night
now exhumed,
bitter blessing of living with no way out.

Fresh virgin roads of rivers
in sleep waver:

and I am still the prodigal, listening
for his name from the silence
when the dead call.

and a space in my heart
is death.

HERMAPHRODITE EARTHWORM

Mild torpor of waters:
the snow yields blue transparencies.

They are memory
of all my hours on earth,
angel hawthorn.

To you I offer myself, threshed
without seed; and within
the saving compassion of meagre leaves
death grieves.

From the mud rises
a pink hermaphrodite
earthworm.

SUFFERED FORMS OF TREES

Now light matures, first fruit of the sun
that wakened it round about
suffered forms of trees,
and the sigh of waters
that night mingled with words;
and raised shades
ply in the hedges.

Futile day
you take me from pendent spaces,
(vacancies, spent deserts)
from calm woodlands
bound round with gold cords,
whose set no rustle of winds
of a sudden subsiding
nor turning of stars changes.

You lay bare my subterranean heart
with its roses and rocking moons,
and wings of beasts of prey
and cathedrals from which dawn
measures the height of planets.

You wake me unknown
to life on earth.

LIVING I SICKEN

I happily breathe on a root
from a rotted tree.

Living I sicken,
and to shed my disease
the flesh suffers too.

AMEN
FOR SUNDAY IN ALBIS

You have not betrayed me, Lord:
I am the first-born
of every grief.

Erato and Apollyon
1932–1936

SYLLABLES TO ERATO

To you the heart in solitude bends,
exile of dim senses
in which it transmutes and loves
what yesterday seemed ours,
and now is buried in night.

Semicircles of air shine
on your face; now you appear to me
in the time when first desires afflict
and you make me white, your mouth relaxed
in the light of your smile.

To have you I lose you,
and I do not grieve: you are beautiful still,
fixed in calm attitude of sleep:
serenity of death the final joy.

SONG OF APOLLYON

Terrestrial night, I was pleased sometimes
at your tiny fire,
and descended among the mortals.

And saw man
lean on the womb of his love
to hear himself being born,
and changed, consigned to earth,
hands clasped,
eyes and mind scorched.

I loved. The hands of the night
creature were cold:
deep terrors she gathered in the vast bed
where in dawn I woke, hearing
the beating of doves.

Then the sky bore leaves
on her moveless body:
the waters rose gloomy in the seas.

My love, I grieve here,
undying, alone.

APOLLYON

The mountains lie inert,
worn out in gloomy sleep.

Apollyon, the hour
of full death is born;
my limbs are sluggish still
and my heart, forgetful, weighs.

I reach out my hands from forgotten
wounds to you,
beloved destroyer.

THE ÀNAPO

At your banks I hear dove water
my Ànapo; to its lamentation
a high rustling
in memory moans.

A youth's form glides
gently up to the shore
from his sport with the gods:

his face mobile,
in the play of light a green growth
swells on his shin.

Leaning over the seething
depths, he suffers again each phase,
bears the nuptial seed of death inside him.

What have you done with the blood's tides
Lord? – Night and the flux of the stars'
returning cycle
vain on his flesh.

A human laugh from barren matter.

Gone down to cool oblivion
he lies in the grasses' dark:
his loved one a shade
listening in his rib.

Docile beasts,
their pupils air,
drink in dream.

DEAD HERON

In the warm swamp, driven into the mud,
dear to the insects, in me
a dead heron grieves.

I am consumed with light and sound;
battered by filthy echoes
from time to time moans a forgotten
breath.

Pity, let me not be
voiceless and without a form
in memory one day.

ON THE HILL OF THE "TERRE BIANCHE"

Outlasting the day
with the trees I abase myself.

A most barren thing,
friend to ailing green,
to cold clouds
resigned in rains.

Sea fills the night,
and the howl sunk in slender flesh
maliciously urges.

An echo of the earth you console us
in the slow torture, beloved;

or the geometric calm of the Bear.

IN YOUR LIGHT I AM WRECKED

I am born in your shipwrecking light,
evening of limpid waters.

The air burns comforted
with serene leaves.

Torn up from the living
I am makeshift heart,
a no-man's-land.

Your terrible gift of
words, Lord, I am
doing my best to repay.

Waken me from the dead:
everyone has his land,
his woman.

You have looked within me
in the darkness of my entrails:
no one holds in his heart
despair like mine.

I am a man alone,
a single hell.

INSOMNIA

Necropolis of Pantàlica

A happy wafting of winged
creatures at odds with green light;
the sea in the leaves.

I am out of tune. And time
rends all that is born to joy in me;
keeps scarcely its echo in voice of trees.

Love for me lost,
memory not human; celestial
stigmata shine on the dead,
starred bodies fall in the rivers;
an hour grows hoarse with gentle rain,
or stirs a song in this eternal night.

For years and years I have been asleep
in an open cell of my land,
shoulders of seaweed against grey waters:

meteors thunder in the unmoving air.

OFTEN A COASTLAND

Often a coastland
beams with solemn stars,
hives of sulphur
sway on my head.

Time of bees: and the honey
is in my throat
still fresh with sound.
A crow wanders at noon
over grey sandstone.

Loved airs, whose calm of sun
teaches of death, and night,
words of sand,

and lost lands of home.

ISLAND OF ULYSSES

Stilled is the ancient voice.
I hearken to fleeting echoes,
deep night's oblivion
in the starry water.

Ulysses' island rises
from the heavenly fire.
Slow rivers bear trees and skies
in the thunder of lunar shores.

The bees bring us gold, beloved:
secret time of the transmutations.

SALT-BED IN WINTER

Sweetness you never rest in me,
assuming a day of limpid light
where all things move
to ordered ends:
you fire the tree in the sky
and the precious smile of human creatures.

Salt-bed; frozen. Once in time
a clear sign was made;
the changing of water
to changeless form
to be in harmony with its laws.

Listen! the cry of young ones shrills,
inhuman the flight of marsh-birds,
in the empty air.

Among scant mosses, in anguish
the livid rock shines out:
adrift on the water
a wrecked root,
a leaf still green,
no use to earth.

SARDINIA

At dayrise lit by the moon,
as you surge out the blue
water moans.

At another mouth
the cry of gulls
breathed more grieving stuff of life.

The same birth was mine:
look, where the ancient islander,
thunder-struck, searches his forehead
for his only eye
and tries his arm,
master in hurling of rocks.

Granite, broken to pieces
by the air; waters that heavy
sleep matures in salt.

Pity has lost me;
and here I find the sign
that speaks of love
to squalid exile
in names of memory: Siliqua
with its slabs of raw earth;
in the bone-piles of stones
in flattened cones.

Transient desert: the shape of your hills
of springing grass thrills in my heart;

and love finds comfort in the friendly breeze.

IN LIGHT OF SKIES

From the pools blessed clouds arise;
the fire of the air, too, will end
in the stilled heart.

Dear time of youth; it is late.
But love I can feel for all earth's things,
in light of skies and shade of wind;
and on every image, the woman
in her green bloom who came to me
not long ago, called by love,
and in whose smile I am mirrored.

So alone I recited my poems
of lost content, and days,
and waters of grassy woodlands
shining in far-off airs.

In this dead island,
abandoned by every heart
that once heard the sound of my voice
I can stay immured.

QUARRIES

Syllables of shadows and leaves:
on the grass the dead
make love, forsaken.

I listen. To the dead, the night is dear,
to me, a mirror of tombs,
of greenest cedar quarries,

of salt mines,
of rivers with Greek names
that sound like melodious verses.

FOR MY MORTAL SMELL

In killed trees
howl the infernos:
summer sleeps in the virgin honey,
the lizard in its monster infancy.

For my mortal smell,
grace to the air of angels
and to water, my heart celestial
in the cell's fertile dark.

IN THE RIGHT HUMAN TIME

In the wind of deep light she lies,
my loved one of the time of doves.
Alone among the living, love,
you talk of waters, leaves and me,
and your voice consoles the naked
night with shining
ardours and delight.

Beauty deluded us, vanishing
of every memory and form,
the lapse and slide revealed to feelings
mirroring the inner splendours.

But from the deeps of your blood with no
pain, in the right human time
we shall be born again.

ALIEN CITY

Another hour falls;
a banana skin opened out like a star
floats on the river. A mixer
drones as it grinds out heaps of stones
on the bay; out by inert barges
yellow sand flows;

and to the arid flow, my grief
that I belie with light-hearted air
each day not mine.

Dead ones alight from lofty hearses
of blood in the fog;
the lamps are touching the pavement.

Black leaves adrift
down long thoroughfares
foretell of wind.

IN THE FEELING OF DEATH

Sky-blue trees
where sweeter sound wanders
and easement rises in the new rains.

On a leafy spray the light
glimmers compliant
in marriage rites with the air;

in the feeling of death,
here I am, fear-struck by love.

OF THE SINNER OF MYTHS

Of the sinner of myths
remember the innocence
O Eternal; and the raptures,
and the deadly stigmata.

He has your sign of good, of evil,
and images over which
the homeland of earth grieves.

New Poems
1936–1942

THE MAGPIE LAUGHS
BLACK IN THE ORANGE TREES

Perhaps it is a true sign of life:
around me children, their heads
light-moving, dance in a game
of lilts and voices on the green
by the church. Mercy of the evening, shades
rekindled on the green of grass,
beautiful in the moon's fire.
wemory allows brief sleep;
Maken now. Listen, the well
roars with the first tide. This is the hour:
mine no more, burnt, distant images.
And you, south wind, heavy with orange scent,
drive the moon on where boys sleep
naked, force the colt out, onto the fields
that are wet with the tracks of mares, open
the seas, lift up the clouds from the trees:
already the heron is moving towards the water
and slowly sniffs the mud among the thorns;
the magpie laughs black in the orange trees.

STREET IN AGRIGENTUM

The wind is still there that I remember
kindling the manes of horses coursing
oblique along the plains; a wind
that stains and gnaws the sandstone and the heart
of the doleful telamons lying
felled on the grass.
Ancient soul grey with bitterness
you return with the wind, sniff
the delicate moss that clothes
the giants thrust down from the sky.
How lonely you are in the space that remains to you;
and greater your grief, if you hear again the sound
as it moves far off and opens out to the sea
where morning Hesperus now creeps.
The marranzano twangs
sad in the carter's throat as he climbs
slow the moon-sharpened hill
in the murmur of saracen olive trees.

THE GENTLE HILL

Far-off birds, open in the evening,
flit on the river. And the rain insists,
and the hiss of poplars lit
by the wind. Like every distant thing
you come again to the mind. The light
green of your dress is here in the trees
burnt by lightning where rises
the gentle Ardenno hill, and the kite-hawk
calls on the broom-corn fans.

Perhaps I cling to that locked-in spiral flight,
deceived in my return –
the harshness, the defeated Christian pity
and this naked penance of sadness.
In your hair is a coral flower
but your face is a shadow that does not change;
(death does this). From the dark
houses of your township I listen
to the Adda, and the rain,
or perhaps a rustle of human footsteps
in the riverbank's tender canes.

WHAT IS IT, SHEPHERD OF AIR?

There again, the call of the ancient
shepherd's horn harsh on the ditches
white with sloughed snakeskins. It blows
perhaps from the uplands of Acquaviva
where Plàtani rolls its shells
under the water among feet of children
with olive skins. Or from what land
bursts the gust of the prisoner wind with its echo
in the light that is crumbling now? What is it,
shepherd of air? Perhaps you are calling the dead.
You who are with me hear nothing, confused with the
sea, the re-echo, tuned in to the low call
of the fishermen hauling their nets.

BEFORE THE STATUE OF ILARIA DEL CARRETO

Now under a tender moon, your hills;
along the Serchio, girls in red
and turquoise dresses lightly move. Dear one
even so in your sweet time, while Sirius
grows pale, and every hour more distant,
and the gull rages on derelict
shores. The lovers walk carefree
in the September air, their gestures
accompanying shades of words
that you know. They have no pity; and you,
held by the earth, what troubles you?
You are left here alone. My shudder
perhaps is yours, of anger and of fear:
remote the dead, and even more the living,
my base and taciturn companions.

NOW DAY IS BREAKING

Night is ended and the moon
melts in the open sky,
sets in the canals.

September is so alive in this land
of plains, the meadows green
as in southern valleys in spring.
I have left my friends,
hidden my heart inside the ageing walls
to remain alone while I remember you.

How remoter than the moon you are
the day now breaking
and hooves of horses clattering on the stones.

THE RAIN IS ALREADY WITH US

The rain is already with us,
shaking the silent air.
The swallows skim dull waters
by the Lombard lakes,
swoop like gulls on the little fish;
there is tang of hay beyond the garden fences.

Another year is burnt,
and no lament, not a cry
raised to win back suddenly one day.

ONE EVENING, SNOW

Far off behind closed doors, I hear
again your mournful animal cry;
so, in the high hamlets under a snow wind
the air moans among the shepherds' folds.

Brief game opposing memory:
the snow has fallen here and gnaws
the roofs, swells the old Lazzaretto arches,
and the Bear plunges red among the mists.

Where is the thigh, colour of my rivers,
the moon's brow within the summer, thick
with murdered wasps? The mourning
of your humbled voice in the darkness of your shoulders
remains, lamenting my absence.

PIAZZA FONTANA

The loved wind lingers no more
in my hair, my brow is deluded:
it bends the docile heads of children
in the square, and of red trees all around.

The human scents
of autumn consume me. And this frenzy
of last summer birds on the Curia
walls is like the grey of its portals,
enduring in air and within
my own calm rustling.

I hear again
the monotonous senile laugh
of migrating sea-birds,
the sudden flapping of doves
that divided the evening, our greeting
on the edges of Hautecombe.

punctual that time humbles itself in symbols,
and this, too, living in its dying.

My power leaves you; quickly
it changes: so on the black wind
of the windows, the fountain water
falls in light rain.

THE TALL SAILING SHIP

When birds came stirring the leaves
of the bitter trees by my house
(they were blind nocturnal winged creatures
drilling their nests in the bark)
I turned my face to the moon
and saw a tall sailing ship.

At the island's lip the sea was salt;
the land stretched out and ancient
shells shone bedded in rocks
in the bay of dwarf lemon trees.

And I said to my love, in whom my child was stirring,
and because of this had always the sea in her soul:
"I am weary of all these wings beating
in time, like oars, and the owls
howling like dogs
when the moon wind is in the canes,
I must go away from this island, leave."
And she: "It is late my dear one, let us stay."

I began then slowly counting
the strong reflections of sea
the air brought to my eyes
from the shape of the tall ship.

ON THE BANKS OF THE LAMBRO

That day vanished from us unblemished
in the water with sailing ships upside down,
the pines left us
(semblance of smoke above the houses)
and the holiday seafront,
with noise in the flags
like ponies neighing.

In the serene hue
that rises here when the moon dies
and sharpens the hills of Brianza
still you move charmed,
pause like a leaf.

The bees dry of honey
climb light with their grain plunder;
already the brightness of the Pleiades is changing.

By the river that now at a wheel's
turn lifts up the empty valley,
childhood, played with the sexes, renews.

I yield myself to its blood
bright on the brow,
its voice enslaved to pain
woeful in the silence of the breast.
All that is left me is already lost:
In the north and east of my island
a wind blows from the rocks
to beloved waters: in spring
it opens the Swabian tombs;
the golden kings deck themselves out with flowers.

An order endures in things,
a semblance of lasting devotion
recalling exile:
on the edge of the rockfall
the boulder hesitates forever,
the root resists the teeth of the mole.
And inside my evening, birds
with tang of orange flit
in the eucalyptus trees.

Here autumn is still in the core
of trees; but the rocks quicken
in the womb of the holding earth,
and long flowers pierce the hedges.
The almost human warmth of hairy corollas
no longer brings revulsion to the mind.

You who are listening smile inwardly:
and suns smoothing the hair
of fleeting girls,
mild joys and hidden fears,
and kindness of resisted tears
rise up again in levelling time!
But autumn-like, your life is hidden.

This night, too, is setting
in the wells of the hills; and the bucket rolls
up to the circle of dawn.
Through the windows trees return
like flowered ships.
                    O dear one,
how far away death was from earth.

EVENING IN THE MÀSINO VALLEY

In the spaces of the hills
all winter, the silence
of the light of sailing ships:
cold image ever
voyaging! Here it revives once more.

The frog soon grows into green,
is a leaf; and the thorn insect
swoops on the herbage of the canals.
The mills try their wheels,
deserted, on yielding water.

I shall hear no more the sea's
roar on the shores of Homeric childhood,
the south-west wind mourning
along the islands at high moon,
women keening the dead, singing
the sweets of marriage days.

And you, like the earth
appear again, sometimes, harsh
and deluding. So little time it takes
to dwindle from living.

In your child's coloured dress
you try a winding step
to the timbrel that sounds like the night
but your face goes vanishing in thuds,
in racked caesuras.

Already the meadows are returning to the valley; loud
the crows lament. What a clear

presence, dear one, of life! In the temples
evening sounds and the signal
is a hollow dialect chant.

Nothing remains of my day.
Weariness surprises me changeless,
pitying every joy that appeared
and hardened so soon at the roots.

Calm night, superior
will of accord
I shall force myself to even such tight measure
of guileless wisdom,
in all the pitiful cold
closed up inside my body.

ELEGOS FOR THE DANCER CUMANI

The wind of the woods
runs bright to the hills.
Day breaks before time: the adolescent,
too, takes fright at the blood.

And the waters' track is dawn
on the shore. The sands' anguish
ebbed out in me to heartbeats,
wandering nightlong.

The ancient, unending cry pains on:
pity for the young creature
death-struck in the grasses
of bitter morning after new rains.

The earth is in that despairing breast,
and there my voice has measure:

you dance to its hidden rhythm
and time returns in fresh formations:
pain too, but turned so to calm
that it burns in sweetness.

In the fast consuming silence
do not throw down this time-bound me,
do not leave me alone in the light;

now that in me you are born
in gentle fire, Anadyomene.

DELPHIC WOMAN

In the air of moon cedars
at the sign of gold we heard the Lion.
The howl of earth was full of portent.
On the temple declining to sleep
the corolla vein is unveiled,
your voice orphic and sea-sounding.

As salt from water
I emerge from my heart.
The age of laurel departs,
its restless ardour
and pity without justice.

The scant contriving of dreams
dies at your naked
shoulder that smells of honey.

O Delphian, I rise in you,·
human no more. Night
of the hot moons' rains

sleeps secret in your eyes:
childhood leaves its non-being
in this tranquillity of ruined skies.

In motions of the starry solitudes,
the bursting grain,
the will of leaves,
you will be my being's cry.

IMITATION OF JOY

Where trees deepen
the evening's abandon
your last step has vanished
indolent, like the flower
that on the linden
barely appears, urging its destiny.

You seek a motive for feeling,
find in your life, silence.
Another fate is revealed for me
by mirrored time. It is pain
like death to see beauty
aflame now in other faces;
lost to me each innocent thing,
even this voice, enduring
in imitation of joy.

HORSES OF MOON AND VOLCANOES

to my daughter

Islands that were my home,
green on a moveless sea.

Dried seaweed and sea fossils
are the beaches where the horses
of moon and volcanoes gallop mating.

In time of landslides
leaves, cranes, assail the air:
by the flood's light shine
dense skies open to the stars;

the doves fly
from the naked shoulders of children.

Here the earth ends:
with work and blood
I make myself a prison.

For you I shall have to throw
myself at the feet of the mighty,
soften my preying heart.

But scorned by men,
still in the flash of light I lie,
a child with open hands,
by trees and river banks:

There the quarry makes fruitful
the Grecian orange tree for the marriage of gods.

AGAIN A GREEN RIVER

Again I am ravaged by a green river,
attunement of grasses and poplars
where sheen of dead snow is forgotten.

And here in the night, sweet lamb
has howled with bloody head:

with that cry floods in the time
of the long wolves of winter,
of the mineshaft, heartland of thunder.

BEACH AT ST ANTIOCHUS

In the clay's bile
and the hiss of snakes
the thick dark rising from the earth
lived in your heart.

And as you grieved to the shoreland skies
you nourished within you
the cruel blood of a lawless race.

Here where the green air of the seas
festers asleep,
an ocean skeleton sticks out white.
And you feel like a pitiful human spine,
pair to the one that the waves
and the salt are wearing away.

For as long as memory comforts
in sighing echoes,
death is forgotten:
And the shining white image on the seaweed
a sign from heaven.

THE MEAGRE FLOWER IS ALREADY FLYING

Of my life I shall know nothing,
mysterious, monotonous blood.

I shall not know whom I loved or love,
now that in March's broken wind
constricted, only my limbs left,
I count the ills of deciphered days.

The meagre flower is already flying
from the boughs. And I watch
the patience of its irrevocable flight.

THRESHOLD OF PUBERTY

Plunderer of languors and pains,
night; a screen for silences,
the age of devious glooms
re-buds in me.

And I see
boys still slender-hipped
at the shell slope
troubled at the change in my voice.

Day after Day
1943–1946

ON THE WILLOW BOUGHS

And we, how could we sing
with a foreign foot on our heart,
among dead abandoned in the squares,
on the grass hard with ice,
to the lamb bleat of children,
the black howl of the mother
going towards her son
crucified on a pole?
On the willow boughs as an offering
even our lyres were hung
and lightly swayed in the sad wind.

LETTER

This silence that hangs in the streets,
this languid breeze that now
slides low among dead leaves, or rises
to the colours of foreign flags...
perhaps the need to say some word to you
before the sky closes again
on another day, or inaction, perhaps,
our basest fault. ... This is not life,
this terrible dark beating of the heart,
this pity; it is no more
than a game of the blood where death is in flower.
O my sweet gazelle, I remember
that geranium of yours bright
on a bullet-riddled wall.
Or does death, even death for love,
no longer console the living?

19 JANUARY 1944

I read you the soft verses of antiquity
and the words, born of the vineyards
and tents on the banks of eastern
rivers – how mournful they fall
and desolate in this blackest night
of war where no one flies
the sky of the angels of death,
and we hear the wind thunder with ruin,
shaking the metal sheets that divide
the balconies up here, and gloom rises
from the dogs howling in gardens
at the rifle shots of patrols
on the empty streets. Someone is alive.
Someone, perhaps, is alive. But we, here,
absorbed in listening to the ancient voice
seek for a sign that outreaches life,
earth's dark sorcery
where even among the tombs of rubble
the vicious grass rears up its flower.

SNOW

Evening falls: again you leave us,
dear images of earth, trees,
beasts, poor people enfolded
in soldiers' greatcoats, mothers
with bellies dried up by tears.
And snow from the fields lights us
like the moon. Ah, these dead ones! Beat
your foreheads, beat right down to the heart.
Let someone, at least, howl in the silence
in this white circle of the entombed.

DAY AFTER DAY

Day after day: damned words, and the blood
and gold. My kind, I know you, monsters
of the earth. At your bite pity has fallen,
and the gentle cross has left us.
I can return no more to my Elysium.
We shall rear tombs by the sea, on the torn fields,
but never one of the graves that mark heroes.
Death has played with us over and over:
there sounded in the air a monotone beating of leaves
as on heathland when in the sirocco wind
the moorhen of the marshes rises up on a cloud.

130

PERHAPS THE HEART

The sharp smell of the limes will drown
in the night of rain. The time
of joy, the frenzy, with its shattering lightning bite
will be vain.
Numbness is all that remains,
a remembered gesture, a syllable,
but like a slow flight of birds
in a haze of mist. And still you wait
for I know not what, my lost one; perhaps
a decisive hour that evokes
the beginning or end: the same fate
from now on. Here the black smoke of the fires
still parches the throat. If you can,
forget that taste of sulphur,
and the fear. Words weary us,
rising again from a flailed water;
perhaps the heart is left us, perhaps the heart.

WINTER NIGHT

And again the winter night,
the village tower dripping dark,
mists engulfing the river,
bracken and thorn-trees. O comrade
you have lost your heart: the plains
have no more room for us.
Here in silence you lament your land:
with wolf's teeth you bite
your coloured handkerchief:
do not awaken the boy who is sleeping beside you,
his bare feet tucked in a cranny.
Let no one remind us of our mothers, no one
tell us a dream of home.

MILAN, AUGUST 1943

In vain you search in the dust,
poor hand, the city is dead.
Dead: on the heart of the Naviglio
the last hum has been heard.
The nightingale has fallen from the flagpole
high on the convent where once he sang before sunset.
Dig no wells in the courtyards,
the living have lost their thirst.
The dead, so red, so swollen, do not touch them:
leave them in the earth of their houses:
the city is dead. Dead.

THE WALL

Already on the stadium wall
in the fissures and clumps of hanging grass
lizards flash by like lightning;
frogs return to the ditches,
a plainsong through my nights in remote
hamlets. You remember this place
where the great star greeted
our shadowy coming. O love, how
much time has dropped with the poplar leaves, how
much blood into the rivers of the earth.

O MY GENTLE BEASTS

Now autumn mars the green of hills,
my gentle beasts. Before night falls
we hear again the birds' last dirge,
the call of the grey plain as it flows
on to the high sounding of sea.
And the smell of wood in the rain, the tang
of holes, how fragrant here
among men and houses, my gentle beasts.
This face that turns slow eyes; this hand
that signs the sky where thunder broods
is yours, my wolves and yours, my foxes,
my gentle creatures burned with blood,
each hand and every face is yours.
And you, you tell me all was wasted,
all the waterworn days of life;
down in the gardens, children singing;
are they then so far away?
They fade upon the air like shadows.
Your voice.
But perhaps I know not all was in vain.

WRITTEN, PERHAPS, ON A TOMB

Here, far from everyone
the sun beats down on your hair, kindling its honey,
and now from its bush the last cicada of summer
and the siren deep-wailing
its warning over the plain of Lombardy
remind us we are alive.
O air-scorched voices, what do you want?
Weariness still rises from the earth.

THIS PILGRIM

So, I return to the silent square:
on your balcony, lonely, flutters the flag
of a bygone holiday.
Reappear, I say. But the echo
from abandoned warrens of stone
deceived only the age that longs for magic.
How long since the unseen stopped replying
when I call, as once before, in the silence!
You are gone. Your greeting no longer
reaches this pilgrim. Joy never
reveals herself twice. And last light
beats on the pine that brings to my mind the sea.
Vain, too, the image of waters.

Our land is far away, in the south,
hot with mourning and tears. Down there
women in black shawls
speak in hushed voices of death,
at the doors of their houses.

FORTRESS OF BERGAMO ALTA

You have heard the cock crow in the air
beyond walls and towers iced with a light
you could not know;
a cry strident with life; the stir
of voices from the cells, and the bird-like
call of the patrol before dawn.
Not a word for yourself
in the constricting net.
And the heron and antelope lost
in a waft of malignant smoke
were mute,
charms of a new born world.
The February moon riding over the earth
was for you no more than a form in the mind
alight in its silence.
You too, among the fortress cypresses
are moving now, soundless; and here
anger calms in the green of the young dead,
and distant pity is almost joy.

BY THE ADDA

By your side at noon the Adda strains along
and you read the reversed shadow of the sky.
Here where the sheep climb up again,
stooping, heads buried in the grass,
the water once flew to the pull of the wheel,
the grind of the olive mill sounded,
and the splash of olives in the tank.
You alone are dismayed at the passing of all that motion.
From the thick of the hedge the elder crown shows
once more, and the canes wave new
leaves on the river reaches.
In this sign from plants is the life that betrayed you,
earth's tender salute to the questions and violence.
For you, the wood's opening renewal in one
blending is certitude, like your blood's conspiring
and the hand you stretch
out and raise to your brow in the sheltering light.

AGAIN I HEAR THE SEA

Many nights now I have heard the sound of the sea
once more, lightly rising and falling on smooth beaches.
A voice's echo shut away in the mind,
rising from time; and, too, this persistent
crying of gulls: perhaps
of tower birds that April
is tempting onto the plains. Once
you, with that voice, were near me;
and I wish now there could come to you
also an echo memory of me,
like that dark ocean murmur.

ELEGY

Cold harbinger of night
returning clear to the balconies
of ruined houses to shine
on unknown tombs, the derelict remains
of the smoking earth. Here rests
our dream. Lonely you turn
north where everything is flowing,
except you only, lightless to death.

OF ANOTHER LAZARUS

From farthest winters the thunder's
sulphurous gong beats on the smoking
valleys. And the voice of the woodlands
as in that time, intones: *Ante lucem*
a somno raptus, ex herba inter homines,
surges. And your stone, where hovers
the image of the world, is thrown aside.

THE FERRY

From where are you calling? The fog
echoes you faintly. It is time;
again from the huts the ravening dogs
leap to the river on the scent:
shining with blood on the far shore
a polecat leers. This is a ferry I know:
there, on the water, black
stones rise up; and all those ships
that pass in the night with sulphur torches.
Already now you are far away
though your voice has the myriad tones of echo,
and I hardly hear its cadence.
But I see you: you have violets clasped
in your hands, so pale, and lichens
near your eyes. So you must be dead.

YOUR SILENT FOOT

Here is the sea, the agave flowering already
the river bright-coloured, flowing
by ancient tombs thick honeycombed in the wall,
and in mirrors, still smiling, girls with dark
unbound hair. There was one at your side
on the Ionic riverbank (a bee
shone honey-smooth in her eye) and she left
barely the light of a name in the olive shade.
No one to be your saviour:
you know that one day dawns like any other
on your face: a quick changing of light
around the circle that surrounds and closes,
beyond the chasm of the moon where
your foot goes silently crossing Hades.

MAN OF MY TIME

You are still the one with stone and sling,
man of my time. You were there in the cockpit,
with evil wings, the sundials of death,
– I have seen you – in the fire-chariot, at the gallows,
at the torture wheels. I have seen you: it was you
with your knowledge precisely extermination-guided,
loveless, Christless. You have killed again
as before, as your fathers killed, as the beasts
killed when first they saw you.
And this blood smells as it did on the day
when the brother said to the other brother:
Let us go into the fields. And that chill, clinging echo
has reached down even to you, within your day.
Forget, O sons, the blood clouds
risen from earth, forget the fathers:
their tombs sink down in the ashes,
the black birds, the wind, are covering their hearts.

Life Is Not Dream
1946–1948

LAMENT FOR THE SOUTH

The red moon, the wind, your
woman-of-the-north colouring, the snow's reaches...
My heart by now is in these meadowlands,
these waters clouded with mist.
I have forgotten the sea, the grave
sound of the shell that Sicilian shepherds blow,
the sing-song of the carts along the roads
where the carob tree shimmers in the haze of stubble fields,
forgotten the passing of herons and cranes
in the air of the green uplands,
for the earth and rivers of Lombardy.
But anywhere man will cry the fate of his homeland.
No one will take me back to the south again.

The south is tired of dragging its dead
on the banks of malarial swamps,
tired of solitude, tired of chains,
tired of the curses in its mouth
of all the races that have howled
death in the echo of its wells,
drunk the blood of its heart.
For this its boys go back into the mountains,
rein in their horses under coverlets of stars,
eat the acacia flowers along the tracks
that are newly red, still red, still red.
No one will take me back to the south again.

And this evening heavy with winter
is ours still, and here I repeat to you
my absurd counterpoint
of gentleness and fury;
a lament of love without love.

145

EPITAPH FOR BICE DONETTI

Her eyes to the rain and spirits of the night,
she is there, in Section Fifteen at Musocco,
the woman from Emilia whom I loved
in youth's sad time.
Death played her off not long ago
while she was quietly watching the autumn wind
from her grey house in the suburbs,
shaking the leaves and branches of the plane trees.
Her face is still vivid with surprise
as it must have been in childhood, thunderstruck
by the fire-eater high on the wagon.
O you who pass, urged on by other dead,
pause for a moment in front of Grave
Eleven-sixty to greet her,
she who never lamented the man
left here detested with his lines,
one like many, worker of dreams.

DIALOGUE

"At cantu commotae Erebi de sedibus imis
umbrae ibant tenues simulacraque luce carentum."
We are filthed with war and Orpheus is aswarm
with insects. He is pitted with lice,
and you – are dead. Winter's iced
weight, the water, the air of storm
were with you, and thunder from echo to echo
throughout your earthly nights. And I know now
that I owed you stronger ties.
But our time has been blood and rage:
others were sinking in the mud,
their hands and eyes in ruin
howling for mercy and love.
Because it is always late to love,
forgive me then. Now I, too, cry out
your name in this noon hour
of lazy wings, strings of cicadas
stretched in the bark of cypress trees.
We no longer know your shore;
there was a pass that poets marked
near rills that smoke with landslides
on the uplands. But there as a boy,
I saw bushes with violet berries,
sheep-dogs and gloomy birds
and horses, mysterious animals
that go behind man, their heads held high.
The living have lost forever
the way of the dead and stand apart.

This silence is more terrible now
than that which divides your shore.
"Frail ghosts went by" – and here
Olona placidly flows. No tree
moves from the well of its roots.

147

O were not you Eurydice? Not Eurydice!
Eurydice is alive. Eurydice! Eurydice!

And you, Orpheus, still foul with war,
like your horse without the whip,
raise high your head, the earth no longer shakes:
howl out your love; conquer the world – if you will.

COLOUR OF RAIN AND IRON

You said: death, silence, solitude,
like love, and life. Words
of our random images.
And each morning the wind rose light,
and time with the colour of rain and iron
passed on the stones
and our muffled drone of the damned.
Truth is still far away.
Tell me, man, split on the cross,
and you with your blood-clotted hands,
how shall I answer those that ask?
Say, now; before other silence
fills up our eyes, before other wind
rises, and other rust flowers.

ALMOST A MADRIGAL

The sunflower bends to the west
and day precipitates in its ruined
eye, and summer's air
thickens, curls already the leaves and smoke
of the builders' yards. The last trick of the skies
fades with the dry glide of clouds and lightning's creak.
Once more, love, as in other years we are held
by the changing trees clustered inside the encircling
canals. But the day is ours still.
It is still that sun that takes its leave
with the thread of its friendly beam.

I have no memories, no wish to remember;
memory springs from death;
life has no end. Each day
is ours. One day will stop forever
and you, with me, when our time seems to grow late.
Here on the canal bank, like children
with feet swinging, we watch the water,
the first branches in its darkening green.
And the man approaching in silence
hides no knife in his hand,
but a geranium flower.

ANNO DOMINI MCMXLVII

You have stopped beating the drums
with a dying fall on all horizons
behind flag-draped coffins, stopped
giving up wounds and tears to pity
in the razed cities, ruin on ruin.
And no one cries any longer "O God why hast
thou forsaken me?" No milk
nor blood flows any more from the riddled breast.
Now you have hidden the guns among the magnolias,
leave us one day without arms, on the grass
with the sound of moving water
and fresh leaves of cane in our hair
while we clasp the woman who loves us.
At nightfall sound no sudden
curfew. A day, a single
day for ourselves, O lords of the earth,
before once again air and metal heave
and a splinter catches us full in the face.

MY COUNTRY IS ITALY

The more the days disperse far off,
the more they return to the hearts of poets.
There are the fields of Poland, there is the Kutno plain
with the hills of corpses burning
in clouds of naphtha; there are the barbed wire fences
for Israel's quarantine,
the bloody refuse, the scorching eruption,
the chains of wretches long since dead,
struck down in the pits their own hands opened;
Buchenwald is there, the gentle beech wood,
with its foul ovens; Stalingrad
and Minsk on its marshes and rotting snow.
Poets do not forget. O multitudes of the abject,
the conquered, the pardoned from pity!
All things revert, but the dead do not sell themselves.
My country is Italy, O alien and enemy;
I sing of its people and their weeping
muffled by the sound of the sea,
the limpid grief of its mothers; I sing of its life.

THÀNATOS ATHÀNATOS

So shall we have to deny you, God
of the tumours, God of the living flower,
and begin with a No to the doubtful
rock "I am", yield to death,
and on every tomb write our sole
certainty: "thànatos athànatos"?
Without a name to recall the dreams,
tears, frenzies of this man
routed by questions that still are open?
Our dialogue alters; the absurd
now becomes possible. There
beyond the smoke of mist, within the trees
the power of the leaves keeps watch,
the river, pressing its banks, is true.
Life is not dream. Man with his jealous
lament of silence is true.
God of silence, lay open solitude.

LETTER TO MY MOTHER

"Mater dulcissima, now the mists are descending,
the Naviglio thrusts disorderly on the locks,
the trees swell with water, burn with snow;
I am not unhappy in the north: I am not
at peace with myself, but seek
pardon from no one, and many owe me tears.
I know you are ailing, live
like all mothers of poets, poor
and just in the measure of their love
for distant sons. Today it is I
who write to you" ... At last, you will say, a line
from the boy who ran away at night
in a skimpy coat with a few lines
of poetry in his pocket. Poor thing, so ready-hearted.
One day, somewhere, they will kill him –
"Yes, I remember that grey stopping place
for slow trains loaded with almonds, oranges,
at the mouth of the Imera, the river full of magpies,
salt and eucalyptus. But now I want to thank you
truly for the wry smile you set
on my lips, a smile as mild as your own:
it has saved me pain and grief.
And if now I shed a tear for you
and all who wait like you and do not know
what they wait for, it does not matter.
O gentle death,
do not touch the clock in the kitchen that ticks on the wall;
all my childhood was passed away on the enamel
of its dial, on those painted flowers:
do not touch the hands, the heart of the old.
Does anyone answer? O death of pity,
death of shame. Goodbye, dear one, farewell my
dulcissima mater."

The False and True Green
1949-1955

THE DEAD GUITARS

My land is on the rivers, hugs the sea;
no other place has such a languid voice
when my footsteps stray
through rushes heavy with snails.
It is autumn indeed: in the wind, in fragments,
the dead guitars pluck the strings
on the black mouth and a hand stirs the fingers
of fire.
      In the moon's mirror,
with breasts like oranges, girls comb their hair.
Who weeps? Who lashes the horses in the red
air? We shall stay on this shore
by the chains of grass and you, love,
do not lead me before that infinite
mirror: boys, singing, and tallest trees
and waters peer there at themselves.
Who weeps? Not I, believe me:
on the rivers dark horses, sulphurous lightnings
race maddened, lashed by a whip.
Not I. My people have blazing
knives, and moons, and wounds that burn.

ENEMY OF DEATH

to Rossana Sironi

Dear one, you should not
have torn your image from the world,
taken from us a measure of beauty.
What shall we enemies of death
do, bent at your rose
feet, your violet chest?
You have left not a leaf, no word
of your last day, no No to all
things of the earth, no No to the monotone
record of man. The sad summer moon
anchor dragged away your dreams:
hills, trees, light, waters,
night; not blurred
thoughts, but true dreams
detached from the mind that fixed for you
at a stroke, the time,
the shame to come. Now
you are closed behind strong doors,
enemy of death. Who is it howling?
You have snuffed out beauty with a breath,
given her the death-blow, ripped her
without a tear for her senseless
shadow spreading above us. Ruined
solitude, beauty, you failed.
You have gestured into the dark, written
your name in the air, your No to all
that swarms here and beyond the wind.
I know what you sought in your new dress.
I know the question that comes back unanswered.
For us there is no reply and none for you,
O moss and flowers, O dear
enemy of death.

THE FALSE AND TRUE GREEN

You wait for me no more with the paltry heart
of the clock. Whether you open or close the gloom,
it does not matter. Thorny, barren
hours are all that remain, with beating
of waste leaves on your windows
high on two streets of clouds.
The slowness of your smile is left me,
the dark sky of a gown, the rust-coloured
velvet binding your hair and
loose on your shoulders; and this, your face
sunk in a water that scarcely stirs.

The beat of coarse and yellowed leaves,
birds of soot. Other leaves now
are splitting the twigs, already bursting
in mesh: the false and true green
of April, the unrestrained sneer
of certain flowering. And you –
you do not flower, sprout days nor dreams
rising from our beyond. Have you lost your child's
eyes, your hands that tenderly
sought my face that eludes me?
For me the shame of writing album
verses, hurling my howls into space,
or into the unbelievable heart that still
struggles with the fragments of its time.

IN A DISTANT CITY

Not from the sky, but steeply down
from foliage onto the lawn
of pale alga in the northern garden, suddenly
a raven hopped. Not a symbol, in the summer
curved over with rainbows and rains, but a real
raven like an acrobat on the trapeze
at Tivoli.
             Fragile, image of cunning
entering our day that ended
with merry-go-rounds and paddle-boat wheels
and sailors' shanties
and the wail of a ship leaving,
opening furious foam wings, or of harbour women's
tears.
           The hour struck on Europe's farthest
shore, insistent, craving
for innocence.
               The raven was still a happy
omen, like others
when I tested my mind in every
one of its bounds and shapes, restraining
a cry to probe the still
world and marvelling that I too
could cry out. Game, perhaps, anticipation
or violence: but for a little irony
all is lost, and the light strikes fear
more than the shade.
                  Were you awaiting my word,
or one unknown to you? Then the raven turned,
lifted its claws swift from the grass
and melted in the air of your green eye.

For a little irony all is lost.

FROM SICILY

HOW LONG THE NIGHT

How long the night, the moon pink and green
to the sound of your call among orange blossoms
when sharp with the dew you knock at a door
like a lord of creation: "Let me in, let me in, beloved."
The wind wrings snatches of hymns and laments
from the Iblei and Madonie peaks
on the timbrels of caves old as the aloe
and the eye of the brigand. And the Bear
stays with you still and shakes the seven
alarm fires lit on the hills,
and the rumble of the red carts of Saracens and Crusaders
stays with you still:
it may be the solitude, the converse, too,
with the starred creatures, the horse,
the dog, the frog; and the delirious
strumming of cicadas in the night.

BEYOND THE WAVES OF THE HILLS

It is not through intrigue, hybrid
signs of the zodiac, or numbers and syllables
arranged to rediscover the world, that life
has eluded you. You have been imprisoned,
measuring with sand and blood
the silences, voices of death,
beyond the waves of the hills.

NEAR A SARACEN TOWER,
FOR MY DEAD BROTHER

I held a gleaming
shell of my sea
and in its faraway sounds I heard
hearts growing with me, beating
a similar age; of gods and beasts, shy ones
and devils: contradictory fables
of the mind. Perhaps the diligent
snap of the dark
traps set for foxes, wolves,
hyenas under the ragged-sailed moon
was for us,
hearts of delicate violets, hearts
of wispy flowers. They should not have risen
and fallen with the sound: the boding thunder
over the rainbow of air and stone
rumbled to the sea's ear
of a childhood astray, dream heritage
warped; and to the earth, of abstract
reckonings where all things
are stronger than man.

TEMPLE OF ZEUS AT AGRIGENTUM

The girl who is sitting on the grass lifts
her coarse hair from the nape of her neck
and laughs at the chase and the lost comb.
The colour says nothing of whether it was wrested
by the burning hand that there in the background
waves from behind an almond tree,
or whether it ended on the mosaic
of the Greek stag by the river brink,
or in a cleft of purple spines.
And the folly of the senses smiles,
and smiles again on the scorching summer
high noon of her island skin,
and the glistening bee buzzes and darts
venom and tender-tacky gums.

In silence we regard this hint
of ironic falsehood: for us the diurnal
moon burns upside down and falls
in the vertical fire. What future is there
to read in the Doric well, what past?
The slow bucket returns from the bottom
with herbs and faces we hardly know.
You turn, shuddering, ancient wheel,
you, sadness, ready preparing
the day in every age, what ruin
you make of angelic images, miracles,
what seas you dash in the narrow light
of an eye! Here is the telamon, a stone's-throw
from Hades (still, sultry-sounding)
stretched in the garden of Zeus, crumbling
his stone with the patience of grubs:
he is here, joint on joint among
trees eternal from a single seed.

WHEN THE WALLS
AND TREES FELL DOWN

LAUDE
29 April 1945

SON:

Mother, why do you spit at a corpse
hanging tied by the feet from a beam, head down:
And the others dangling beside him, don't they
disgust you? Ah! that woman with the ghoulish can-can
stockings, and mouth and throat of trampled
flowers! No, mother, stop! Shout
to the crowd to go. This is not grief but leering
and joy. The horseflies are glued already
to the knots of veins. Now you have aimed at that face:
mother, mother, mother!

MOTHER:

We have always spat at corpses, son:
hanging from window-bars and masts of ships,
burnt at the stake, torn to pieces
by hounds at the edge of estates for the sake of a little
grass. An eye for an eye, a tooth
for a tooth, turmoil or quiet, no matter:
after two thousand years of eucharist
our heart wants open the heart that opened yours
my son. They have gouged your eyes, maimed
your hands, just for a name to be betrayed.
Show me your eyes, give me your hands:
you are dead, son, and because you are dead, my son,
you can pardon, my son, my son.

SON:

This sickening, sultry heat, this smoke
of ruins, the fat green flies bunched on the hooks:
justly the anger and blood are flowing.
Not for you, mother, and mother, not for me:
tomorrow they will pierce my eyes and hands
again. All down the ages pity
has been the howl of the murdered.

TO THE FIFTEEN OF PIAZZALE LORETO

Esposito, Fiorani, Fogagnolo,
Casiraghi, you names, who are you? Ghosts?
Soncini, Principato, you, Del Riccio,
Temolo, Vertemati, Gasparini,
dead inscriptions? Galimberti, Ragni,
you, Bravin, Mastrodomenico, Poletti,
leaves of a tree of blood?
Dear blood of ours that does not soil the earth,
blood that initiates the earth
in the hour of rifle fire.
We are shamed by the bullet wounds in your backs;
too long has passed. Death falls again
from funeral mouths; the foreign
flags still hanging over your houses
are asking for death. Believing they are alive
they fear death at your hands.
The watch we keep is no mourning,
no vigil of tears at your tombs;
death that is life can cast no shadow.

AUSCHWITZ

Far from the Vistula, along the northern plain,
love, in a death-camp there at Auschwitz:
on the pole's rust and tangled fencing, rain
funeral cold.
No tree, no birds in the grey air
or above our thought, but limp
pain that memory leaves
to its silence without irony or anger.

You wish for no elegies or idylls: only
the meaning of our destiny, you, here,
hurt by the mind's war,
uncertain at the clear
presence of life. For life is here
in every No that seems a certainty:
here we shall hear the angel weep, the monster, hear
our future time
beating the hereafter that is here, forever
in motion, not an image
of dreams, of possible pity.
Here are the myths, the metamorphoses.
Lacking the name of symbols or a god,
they are history, earth places,
they are Auschwitz, love. How suddenly
the dear forms of Alpheus and Arethusa
changed into shadow-smoke!

Out of that hell hung with a white
inscription "Work will make you free"
there came the endless smoke
of many thousand women thrust at dawn
out of the kennels up to the firing-wall,
or, screaming for mercy to water, choked,

their skeleton mouths under the jets of gas.
You, soldier, will find them in your annals
taking the forms of animals and rivers,
or are you too, now, ash of Auschwitz,
medal of silence?
Long tresses in glass urns can still be seen
bound up with charms, and an infinity
of ghostly little shoes and shawls of Jews:
relics of a time of wisdom,
of man whose knowledge takes the shape of arms,
they are the myths, our metamorphoses.

Over the plains where love and sorrow
and pity rotted, there in the rain
a No inside us beat;
a No to death that died at Auschwitz
never from that pit of ashes
to show itself again.

TO THE CERVI BROTHERS, TO THEIR ITALY

In all parts of the earth base minds are sniggering,
princes and poets, re-hashing the world in dreams,
sages in malice, thieves of knowledge.
In my country, too, they laugh at pity,
the patient heart, the lonely despair of the poor.
And my land is shining with men, and trees, and martyrs,
shapes in colour and stone, and ancient meditations.

Foreigners tap your saints on the chest, your loving
relics, with salesmen's fingers, drink your wine
and incense under the strong moon of your shores:
they tune on guitars of kings the chant of volcanoes.
For countless years they have sent their armies in,
slipped from the hills to the plains with the rivers and cattle.

Here in the night's tenderness Polyphemus is weeping
still for his eye that a far island seaman
put out. And the olive stake is still red-hot.

Here, too, they separate nature into dreams,
dress up in death, laugh, the familiar enemies.
Some were with me in the time of solitude
and love poems in the confused anguish of slow mill-stones
and tears. Their story came to an end in my heart
when walls and trees crashed to the ground amid rage
and brotherly grief in that city of Lombardy.

But I am still writing words of love, and even
this is a letter of love to my native land.
I write to the Cervi brothers, not to the seven
stars of the Plough: to the seven Emilian men

of the fields. There were few books in their hearts; they
    died
throwing dice of love, in silence. Soldiers, philosophers,
poets, knew nothing of this kind of peasant Humanism.
Love, Death, in a shallow grave of mist.

Every country covets your names of modesty
and strength, not for remembrance, but for the days that flow
slow in history, swift in engines of blood.

EPIGRAMS

TO A HOSTILE POET

to Giuseppe Marotta

On the straw-coloured sands of Gela
as a child I would lie by the ancient
Grecian sea, many dreams in my breast
and my clenched fists. Exiled Aeschylus there
scanned over his verses and lines forlorn
in the burning gulf where the eagle spied him
that final day. Man of the North who wish me
nothing, or dead, hope for your own peace:
next spring my father's mother will be
a hundred years old. Hope that tomorrow I
shall not be playing with your rain-yellowed skull.

FROM THE WEB OF GOLD

From the web of gold foul spiders hang.

The Incomparable Earth
1955–1958

VISIBLE, INVISIBLE

VISIBLE, INVISIBLE

Visible, invisible
the carter on the horizon
calls out in the arms of the road,
replies to the voice of the islands.
And I, too, keep a straight course;
the world rolls on all round, and I read
my history as a nightwatchman
the hours of rain. The secret has happy
margins, guiles, difficult attractions.
My life, you cruel, smiling
denizens of my ways and landscapes, has no
handles to its doors.
I do not make myself ready for death;
I know the beginning of things.
The end is a surface where
the invader of my shadow travels.
I don't recognize shadows.

THE INCOMPARABLE EARTH

I have long owed you words of love:
perhaps those that vanish each day
as soon as struck, feared by memory
that changes the inevitable signs to hostile
dialogue, battering the soul.
Perhaps the mind's sinking drowns my loving
words, or fear of the random echo clears even
the weakest image of its loving sound;
or they touch the hidden irony, its hatchet
nature, or my life, hemmed in already, love.
Or perhaps it is colour that dazzles them,
clashing with the light
of the time that will come to you when mine
can call no more to love, dark
love, already weeping
the beauty, the violent rupture
with the incomparable earth.

TODAY, THE TWENTY-FIRST OF MARCH

Today, the twenty-first of March, the Ram
enters the equinox and beats
his male head against trees and rocks,
and you, love, at his blows
loosen the winter wind
from your ear as you turn to hear
my latest word. The first
foam floats on the plants, pale,
almost green, and accepts
the signal. The news speeds on, up
to the gulls as they meet
in the rainbows: out they well,
their call hissing
with the spray that chimes
in the caverns. Their cries are drowned
by yours, beside me, opening the bridge
between us and the squalls
that nature prepares underground
in a headstrong flash.
You outstrip the thrust of the buds;
now we need more than spring.

FROM DISFIGURED NATURE

The symmetrical leaf
flees from disfigured nature, the anchor
no longer holds. Already winter, not winter,
and a bonfire smokes by the Naviglio.
By that night fire
one could betray, deny the earth
three times. How strong its hold
if for years, such years, you have looked
without loathing at the dirty stars
floating in the canals, if you love
someone on earth, if the fresh wood
crackles, and the crinkled geometry
of the leaves warms you as it flames.

AN OPEN ARC

Evening shatters in the earth
with thunder of smoke and the owl
beats out "tu", telling only
of silence. The high dark islands
crush down the sea; on the beach
night enters inside the shells. And you
measure the future, the beginning
no longer here, part and slowly break up
the sum of a time already missing.
As the foam clings to the stones you lose the sense
of the ruin's impassive flow.
The closed song of the owl
knows no death as it dies,
feels around in its hunt for love, continues
an open arc, reveals
its solitude. Someone will come.

A COPPER AMPHORA

On the hedge the thorns
of the prickly pears, your new
blue petticoat torn, anguish
deep in your gouged-out heart,
at Lentini, perhaps, near Iacopo's place
in the marshes, learned counsel on eels
and loves. What story does the earth
tell, the trilling of blackbirds
hidden in the noonday famishing
for fruit hard with violet
and ochre-coloured seeds. Your hair
tempestuous over your ears
that no longer hear,
watercolour hair, its colour lost.
A copper amphora at a doorway
glistens with drops of water
and red wisps of grass.

TO MY FATHER

Where Messina was on the violet
waters among broken
wires and ruins you walk the rails
and points with your cap like an island
cock. The earthquake for three days now
has been boiling. It is December
of hurricanes and poisoned sea. Our nights
fall in the goods wagons: we are young cattle
counting our dusty dreams with the dead
flattened by iron, nibbling almonds
and apples dried in garlands. The science
of pain brought truth and knives
to our games on the flatlands of yellow
malaria and mud-swollen tertian fever.

Your sad, delicate
patience took away our fear,
was a lesson of days linked to the death
betrayed, the contempt of thieves
caught in the rubble and executed in the dark
by firing squads from the landing parties, a bill
of small figures that worked out dead
right, a measure of life to be.
Your sun cap used to go to and fro
in the little space they always gave you.
For me, too, they measured everything
and I have borne your name
a little further than the hate and envy.

That red on your cap was a mitre,
a crown with the wings of an eagle:
and now in the eagle of your ninety years
I have wanted to speak, your departure
signals coloured by the night-light,

179

here, from the world's faulty wheel
in a mass of crowding walls
far from the Arabian jasmine
where still you are, to say
what once I could not – hard
kinship of thoughts –
as the keeper says to his master,
(the agave lentisk, the marsh cicadas are not
the only ones who are listening)
"I kiss your hands." This: and no more.
Life is mysteriously strong.

THE TOMBS OF THE SCALIGERS

Heroes now are fossils, debated
in the museums of history – soldier,
soldier-bee, dying on the verge of truth – and man
becomes a hero through guile and injustice;
schedules and drafts of his daily glory one
by one are handed down through the ages,
the ones marked with the sign of Christ or the Devil.
I turn and salute your tomb, Cangrande
della Scala, even though your corpse, still
intact, vanished to purple, princely dust
in the air and the River Adige. Between
the geranium sign of the Moors' alley
and the white drapers' shops you were,
raised up from the ground,
in a covering bound to disintegrate
without rains and silt of the hard rock. Yet
for thousands of years my forebears drew
their dead up high and led them away
in the cells of the beehive tombs of Pantàlica.
Nearer the sky, Cangrande, and the shining
imagination of the stars: further away
from the earth man fears, alive or dead.

AN ACT OR A NAME OF THE SPIRIT

Pirate life, you have raised the grand ensign,
entering my sea, to bloody and scatter
under the beating edge of your battleaxe
my hopes, my selfhood between dream
and invisible day. The cricket
in the poppies, and the dormouse clinging on the beeches
are vanished, the stringed instrument, the speaking
lyre of the bards; but not the myths,
guardians of thoughts. And courtly
love was of long duration with rough
judgements and frenzies. I look from a hill
of tufa and shells and my gaze
patrols the sea, full of childish rancour.
You have stripped me of all my firstborn rights,
with your camps pitched under my soul.
But even if you with your omens had given a friendly
greeting to my stones, to my beasts and my trees,
I would not have altered a single inner word
of my past or future. Not even you
decide an act or a name of the spirit,
coarse pirate
of prudence, unending madness.

STILL OF HELL

THE WALL

Against you they are raising a wall
in silence, stone and lime, stone and hate,
each day from loftier zones
they lower the plumb-line. The masons
are all alike, small, spiteful,
dark of face. On the wall
they mark slogans about the world's
duties, and if the rain erases them
they write them again with still more ample
geometries. Every so often someone crashes
from the scaffolding, and another immediately
runs to his place. They are not dressed in blue
denim, and they talk a pointed jargon.
The rock wall is high;
in the beam sockets lizards
and scorpions now weave, black weeds
hang. From one horizon only, the sheer
dark bulwark avoids the earth's
meridians, and the sky does not cover it.
You, on the other side of this bastion,
ask neither grace nor confusion.

IN THIS CITY

In this city there is even a machine
that grinds out dreams; with a quick
counter, a little disc of pain
you're sent in a moment, on this earth,
unknown in the midst of frenzied shadows
on phosphorous seaweed, mushrooms of smoke:
a roundabout of monsters
revolving on shells
that shatter to rotten pieces as they play.
It's in a bar down there at the bend
of the plane trees, here in my city
or elsewhere: come on, the switch is already thrown.

STILL OF HELL

You will not tell us, one night, shouting
through megaphones one night
of births' orange blossoms and loves only just
beginning, that hydrogen in the name
of right is burning the earth. Woods, animals, melt
in the Ark of destruction, the fire
is a lime on the horses' skulls,
in human eyes. Then to us dead
you dead will state new codes
of law. In the ancient tongue,
other signs, outlines of daggers.
Someone will stutter over the dross,
discover everything over again
or nothing in the uniform lot,
the murmur of streams, the light's
crackle. Of hope you dead
will not speak to our death, in the funnels
of boiling mud,
here in hell.

NEWS ITEM

Claude Vivier and Jacques Sermeus,
old friends of high-walled orphanage days
coldly, with a revolver, for no reason
murdered two young lovers in a car
standing in the Saint-Cloud park
along the Avenue de la Félicité
at the edge of dusk
on the twenty-first of December,
nineteen hundred and fifty six.
Claude Vivier says the crime
was for small stakes, and requests, black
spider and bird, before the guillotine,
Landru's or Weidmann's cell
in the prison of Versailles. The two
youths are intelligent and tough.
We have to save the civilized impulses,
the cavern's happy solitude, most ancient
latins. Envy of love, hatred
of innocence; formulae of the soul.
Hope always has a tight-gripped heart,
and we shall have others like Claude and Jacques,
though we do not know the number, the golden
balance between debit and credit of mankind.

ALMOST AN EPIGRAM

The contortionist in the bar, a melancholy
gypsy, suddenly gets up
from a corner and offers a quick
performance. He takes off his jacket
and in his red sweater bends over
backwards and like a dog
snatches in his mouth
a soiled handkerchief. He repeats the back-bending
twice more in shirtsleeves and then bows
with his plastic dish. He wishes us
a good win on the Pools, and vanishes.
The atomic age is at its height.

SOLDIERS WEEP BY NIGHT

Neither the Cross, nor childhood, the scourge
of Golgotha, the angelic memory,
are enough to root out war.
Soldiers weep by night
before dying, they are strong, they fall
at the feet of the words they learnt
under the arms of life.
You account for lovers, soldiers,
nameless torrents of tears.

FROM GREECE

AT NIGHT ON THE ACROPOLIS

One night at Athens in the white sea
of the Acropolis an owl said Athena.
It was not a spiteful call, the moon
too white, the granite hard foam;
and the olive tree near the Erechtheum
marked slanting waved triangles,
crabs in motion. The owl sounded
over the sea, happy and fresh. Beasts
with white blood in their trunks stirred the columns.
Composed bird, the owl revolves its meditations,
a melodic ellipse with beak
merged and perfect. The guide said
from his wave of moon
that in the centre of the Parthenon
the explosion of a Turkish magazine
shattered the harmony of the masses,
spoke of the downfall of Pallas Athena,
the advent of Maria
Virgin mother, daughter of her *son*
on the wooden horn of the yellow owl.

MYCENAE

On the Mycenae road with its eucalyptus
trees you can find resiny
wine and cheese of sheep's milk "À la belle
Hélène de Ménélas", a tavern
that leads thought away from the blood
of the Atridae. Your palace, Agamemnon,
is a bandits' hide-out under Mount
Zara, of stone unscratched by roots,
perched over twisted ravines
The poets speak much of you, of the crime
invented in your house of crises,
of Electra's sombre frenzy,
for ten years drawing her distant
brother to matricide with the eye
of her sex; the diabolical speak
of the queen's logic – wife
of the absent soldier Agamemnon,
mind, sword betrayed.
And you alone are lost
Orestes, your face vanished without
a golden mask. To the Lions of the gate,
and skeletons of the scenic harmony
raised by philologists of the stones,
greetings from a Greek Sicilian.

FOLLOWING THE ALPHEUS

The harmonies of the earth,
the sound of the clay,
rust of the bullrushes, low green
leaves on the banks of Alpheus
near Olympia of Zeus and Hera,
but more than all this unison, signs within
of a stubborn ruin, the oddness
of strange contrasts: relics, after all,
of negations defended like life.
And the harmony of your waters does not matter,
Alpheus, you are calm here, silent
in Elis; on the pebbles wavers
a chrysalid sun
that seems as if it will set by stealth
after so long a flight. I seek only
discords, Alpheus,
something more than perfection.
I long to turn away from Olympia now,
from its interweaving of pines, still forms
rejected by death, to move beyond
the confined vault that I know. A door
to burst open, Olympia, haunt of learning
and tourists; a robber's leap
on the most fiery horse from one of the pediments
is needed. I am not in search of a haunt
of childhood, following the river back under the sea,
there by the fountain of Arethusa
to tie up the link
broken by my arrival:
the blurred, calm continuance,
Olympia, like Zeus, like Hera.
I survey your detached head on the grass,
with a moon of burning straw.

191

DELPHI

A plant, neither laurel
nor myrtle, common stem
and leaves where soul
and body can graft themselves for metamorphosis
to prove there is no death
even at Delphi.
There is no laurel for the oracle
and no cave for the sortilege. The sun
pants down from Parnassus, unhinging
this centre of the world. The Castalian fountain drips
warm on the tourists' lips
and the vendor of mineral water laughs
near the spring with its two votive
statues damp with mould. On the first step
of the temple, Phoebus,
if he knows you, raises his bow
and shoots straight at the sinews,
hidden under the channel of stones
where the sacred serpents breed.
And whether inertia is life, and death
motion, one can no longer say.
Here on the stadium
from the silver groins of the hills, with their sharp
    moon curves
the plebeian charioteer forever departs
with his low brow and glazed grasshopper eye.

MARATHON

The lament of the mothers at Marathon,
the cry from the people's bowels
went unheard by any. Greece
was free. Free Greece is.
Marathon is a place of soldiers
not sibyls; there rises up here neither temple
nor altar. Its tumulus is intact. From up there
Euboea can be seen. Grub of history,
everything on the site tones in,
here the pillar, in the earth, helmet and sword;
and despite this Marathon of Marathons
the men on the plains of Argos live
in houses like sentry boxes.

MINOTAUR AT KNOSSOS

The young Cretans had slim
waists and rounded flanks. The Minotaur
bellowed in the Labyrinth for them too.
Knowledge, Ariadne, of Pasiphaë's lusts
who foamed out bestial likenesses with the bull
sprung up like Venus from the sea.
But art, the trappings of man, the finer
signs of a cultured living
are yours, Cretans; there is no death.
But no one is left to knife
the monster at Knossos, and at Heraklion
in the market's oriental dirt and disorder
there is nothing that resembles
the Greece that was before Greece.

193

ELEUSIS

At Eleusis a general has erected
a tower in cement and lead,
with a clock that at night beats out
the signs of the mysteries. From its orbit
the hours make a coarse, dull vortex
on the stone where once in cadence
the funeral record knelled the monotonous
appearing of the dead. The lone archon
trampled Eleusis,
its wicker baskets full of vigorous
symbols, big with human wailings,
sticking his snout in the black pearls
on Hades' invisible arch.
There Aeschylus spoke to lunar Hecate:
What good is there,
what is there without ill?

QUESTIONS AND ANSWERS

٠

TO THE NEW MOON

In the beginning God created the heaven
and the earth, and in due time
set moon and stars in the heavens;
and on the seventh day he rested.

After a thousand ages, man,
made in his image and likeness,
without ever resting, with his
lay intelligence
one October night, without fear,
set in the tranquil heavens
other bodies like those
that had been spinning
since the creation of the world. Amen.

AN ANSWER

Though the anchor of Ulysses burns in the mind,
here on the shore of Acis' sea, among boats
with black eyes on the prows to ward off evil
fate, if I could, from the nothingness of the air,
here, from the nothingness that shrieks on a sudden
and grapples like the swordfish spear,

from the nothingness of the hands that change
like Acis, shape from the nothingness a living
ant, and push it into the sandy
cone of its labyrinth, or a virus
to give eternal youth to my most
dedicated enemy,
perhaps, then I would be like a God –

in the equal sureness of life
and death not as opposites:
here wave and lava, phantoms
of the light of this already future
bright winter morning – an answer
to a due of nature, and an anguish
that flames on a milestone number,
the first on the burning road
that burrows into the beyond.

ANOTHER ANSWER

But what for the love of Christ do you want?
Nothing happens in the world and man
still tightens his raven's wings
on the rain and proclaims love and discord.
For you there has always been blood
since time began. Only the sheep
turned round on its way back with scrawny
head and eyes of salt.
But nothing happens. And the chronicle
on the walls of the city of a distant archipelago
is already mossed over.

TWO INSCRIPTIONS

are now published for the first time.
The "Inscription for the Fallen of Marzabotto"
was discovered on 3 October 1954
at the base of the "Faro del Martirio",
built on a promontory near Marzabotto.

INSCRIPTION FOR THE FALLEN OF MARZABOTTO

This is a memorial to blood
of fire, to martyrdom,
to the vilest extermination of people,
ordained by Von Kesselring's nazis
and their mercenary soldiers
in the last days of Salo's subjection,
as a reprisal against partisan action.

The one thousand eight hundred and thirty people of
    the plateau
shot and burnt,
from humble peasant and working-class stock,
enter the history of the world
with the name of Marzabotto.
Terrible and just their glory:
civil consensus demonstrates
to the powerful the laws of the right
to govern even the heart of man:
it asks neither pity nor anger,
but instead the honour of free arms
in the presence of the woods and hills
where Lupo and his band
many times threw back
liberty's enemies.

Their death covers an immensity of space
wherein men of every land
remember Marzabotto,
its savage age
of barbarity in our time.

1954

INSCRIPTION FOR THE PARTISANS OF VALENZA

This stone
commemorates the partisans of Valenza
and those who fought in its earth,
fallen in action, shot, assassinated
by Germans and provisionals of the Italian militia.
Their number is vast.
Here we count them tenderly, one by one,
calling them by names
that are green forever.
Curse not, eternal alien in your country,
and you, friend of liberty, salute.
Their blood is fresh still, silent
its fruit.
Heroes have become men: a blessing
for civilization. With men like these,
Italy, may you never be poor.

1957

Debit and Credit
1959–1965

DEBIT AND CREDIT

Nothing, you give me nothing, you
who are listening. The blood
of the wars has dried.
Contempt is a pure desire
provokes no response
from a human thought
outside the hour of pity.
Debit and credit. In my voice
there is at least a sign
of living geometry;
in yours a dead
shell with funeral dirges.

VARVÀRA ALEXANDROVNA

A dry birch branch with the green
inside beats on a vortex window
of Moscow. At night Siberia looses its shining
wind on the scumbled pane, a web
of abstract thoughts in the mind. I am sick:
it is I who could die any minute;
    really I, Varvàra Alexandrovna, doing the rounds
of the Botkin in felt slippers
with your hurrying eyes, nurse of fate.
I am not afraid of death,
have not been afraid of life.
Or I think someone else is stretched out here.
Perhaps if I do not remember love, pity, the earth
that breaks indivisible nature, the livid
sound of solitude, I can fall from life.
Your nocturnal hand is burning, Varvàra
Alexandrovna; they are my mother's fingers
squeezing to leave long peace
under violence. You are human Russia
of Tolstoy or Mayakovsky's time;
you are Russia, not a landscape of snow
in a hospital mirror;
you are a multitude of hands seeking out other hands.

ONLY IF LOVE SHOULD PIERCE YOU

Do not forget that you live in the midst of the animals,
horses, cats, sewer rats
brown as Solomon's woman, terrible
camp with colours flying,
do not forget the dog with harmonies of the unreal
in tongue and tail, nor the green lizard, the blackbird,
the nightingale, viper, drone. Or you are pleased to think
that you live among pure men and virtuous
women who do not touch
the howl of the frog in love, green
as the greenest branch of the blood.
Birds watch you from trees, and the leaves
are aware that the Mind is dead
forever, its remnant savours of burnt
cartilage, rotten plastic; do not forget
to be animal, fit and sinuous,
torrid in violence, wanting everything here
on earth, before the final cry
when the body is cadence of shrivelled memories
and the spirit hastens to the eternal end;
remember that you can be the being of being
only if love should pierce you deep inside.

A SEPTEMBER NIGHT

"Timor mortis conturbat me"?
A drum beats hollow
in the foreign night
on knots of blood. Crows fall
in the snow hit by a silent
bullet. And suddenly my body
climbs up an orange tree sheer
on the Ionian Sea. But you are here, at the end,
no meeting sign at the spirit's
surrender, along with yourself, you listen
to far-off thoughts, the last
ones hanging under a gothic vault.
In what place, underground shades?
Death is the same as oneself;
a door opens, a piano is heard
on the television in the drug-tented
ward. Into the mind there comes
a dialogue with the beyond,
of spiralling syllables winding
requiem on curves of dark; .
an involuntary yes or perhaps.
I owe no confessions to the earth,
nor to you, death, beyond your
door open onto the video of life.

ALONG THE ISAR

to Annamaria Angioletti

Another foreign city: the evening crumbling,
the houses dunes in the seaweed
light on every neon keel,
and I respond as if
the Isar were a river of my island.
Someone sings from the taverns
to a guitar, in boredom perhaps, or anger.
The mind's beam reverses, probing steep
contours of my history
where I trample what I most desire.
Mute recruits of Sunday descend
to the river. But where are your
drums beating, love? Here the rain
unfrosts, floats in the reflections
and I think of you hearing
as from immense trees, dissonances,
tears, fickle echoes, residues
of meditations within my body
and the noise of death in its unalternating
arc and my urgent, stifled
question. To be as I could be.
The wind lifts shining grey eddies
from the water: here tomorrow
I shall speak my heart to the Bavarians
and you
know that I speak to you on the Naviglio
of thwarted landscapes, appearances
of the future which I envy here on earth.

FROM THE SHORES OF THE BALATON

At Balatonfüred a young lime tree
bears my name. The heart-shaped
leaves reach out along the shores far
from their homeland. Each year my friend Szabó
(one night on the Danube I recited to him
the lines of the Greek Diodorus of Sardis
on Aeschylus who rests near the white
waters of Sicilian Gela through envy
of the Athenians) when summer
comes, reminds me of my days
in Hungary from his lake with two leaves
of the tree, ghosts that arrive still
fresh-veined in the land of Lombardy.
The lime tree grows in its green calendar leaves.
As soon as it is high enough to be a sea-birds'
perch, and under its branches holiday-makers
bent over oil-cloths in red and blue
squares drink carafes of Tokay,
a loudspeaker suddenly
empty of sounds
will say my name, free, from the beyond.
Like a warning of rain squalls.

TOLLBRIDGE

To a saltpetre sun grey with mistral
the gulls of Tollbridge
cry under Sognefiord's iron arch
that repeats plans of escape
to the air thrown on its thin
gratings. The North leaps on the islands
of barbarous stone, incites its monsters
with real images, squeezes the apple tree's
sap in its long
nocturnal day. Sameness of light
on the colours of the wooden houses
and the hedges of bristling barbed wire.
How far I can count my future
on the screen of impassive
initials, appearances!
In this defiled forever,
in a space of boulders, Norwegian
trees, I do not shriek in fear
to nature that crashes
as I seek a time without form.

THE NEGRO CHURCH AT HARLEM

The negro church at Harlem
is on the first floor of a house and seems
an *atelier*. One enters as if to buy
a fetish or a sacred souvenir.
The place has an altar embellished
like certain sweets of the South with round
spots in yellow, blue, and red.
The priest prays in silence
with white eyes like the black-skinned
girls who will fall in a trance
in the anguish of the Christian God. One, two,
entered into by the invisible breath, dance
headlong, staggering east and west,
genuine crucifixions, vanquished and vanquishing,
armed with their detached souls.
The possessed ones sing; God watches them
from baroque clouds in the smell of human
candles lit by hope and pain.

CAPE CALIAKRA

Along the Bulgarian Dobruja on clay
roads and tight rock splits
of dead fiords edged on the Black Sea
near the tower of a military beacon
the granite of Caliakra sinks.
The forms spring from the water in Turkish
crescents. The seals gambol, roll,
vanish billowing in the holed
surf. I do not listen to legends or myths
of a world of lost races,
of seamen, corsairs. Here
one can separate inner from outer, work
the mind beyond the ferocious
landscape, hear the sound of a water-pump,
an unfriendly dog barking, take a flower
cut by the wind, refuse the buzzing
of a rhyme, alien to the beacon light
that begins its trials of feeble fire.
The time is not ended, no one tells me
of the tricks of nature, balances,
laws. Not even you Caliakra, beetling
over gulls, and seals offered to the high coast.

THE SILENCE DOES NOT DECEIVE ME

Garbled, the beating
of San Simpliciano's bell
assembles on my window-panes.
The sound has no echo, takes a transparent
circle, brings to mind my name.
I write words and analogies, try
to trace a possible link between
life and death. The present is outside me,
will only in part be able to contain me.
The silence does not deceive me, the formula
abstract. What must come is here,
and if, love, it were not for you,
the future would already have that echo
I do not want to listen to, quivering as
sure as an insect of earth.

GLENDALOUGH

The dead of Glendalough
under the Celtic crosses look from a hill
flowing with short black
clouds. They say they are running from spring,
listen idly to the rain's
downpour and ghosts of the crows
sifting and following white westerly
words up there. They are friends
these dead in the gullies,
friends of the sea that further off
bends under blizzards, embedding
the moon in the waves. The Celts' names
are of alarms and illusory thunderings.
Near a torrent, in the sun,
there was no storm, nor the romantic
twilight of mid-day,
and only a crow leered
from the sky, remembering a most beautiful Lady
who died of love inside the convent of Kevin
with the funnel-shaped roof.

TUSCAN CROSSBOWMEN

Dressed up in gay brocades the bowmen
in the Tuscan city square
without victorious drums, try
their luck at hitting a bull's-eye
with medieval arrows. The youths
strain back the bow-strings, launch
their bolts with the eagerness of lovers.
Rapid, they repeat the spell,
I was with you, love; the blows
on the target, in the sharp meridian
light, the tedium
of waiting for those serfs of the ancient
war, told us that man does not die;
he is a soldier of love, of unending victory.

IN CHISWICK CEMETERY

Resonances of myrtles
in the green precinct of ancient
dead, where Foscolo laid his head
inside a sarcophagus in a time
of love for the English. His stone bears
the date of birth and death. Opposite
at the bend of the road strong beer
is drunk in a timber pub
with nordic eaves. A wheel
turns, on a table an old man beats
with a hammer. The love for Foscolian ghosts
is stronger here than in Santa Croce – still
in the armour of exile. The weak-kneed Lombard brutes
sharpened up spears and axes, measured
man on the jambs of the doors
as an object useful in arms.

THE MAYA AT MÉRIDA

The rain at Mérida falls hot
and dark on the Maya, with brackish syllables
outside the porticos. People
of age-old weeping,
refined ambitions. Small men
with compact rippling shoulders.
They stand in front of the ice-cream and
cake shops, sniffing
the fat fried between sheets of old
papers and rinds of tropical fruits.
Antique, rejected, ironic or
grotesque like the dwarf sculptures
that stand at the corners and in the portals
of Romanesque churches. Never again to return
among men, cast into an infinite
lassitude. Never again; scattered, scarred,
they recount their dreams asleep on old
benches in public gardens,
in the churches during Mass, sprawled
free in their rags. America,
Spain, watch them in that rotting South
their carcasses breaking up like gods of death.

WORDS TO A SPY

There is a spy who writes
love poems in my city. His feet
rise along the shop windows,
the hopeful pavements.
You crawled once
on the face of your dead,
those who nailed themselves to the walls
for one kind secret word from you
in the code of leading rhymesters.
Spies can't write poems, you know,
nor drink wine with friends, nor speak
words to anyone's heart.
The earth is quick, you have no roots,
I know your name, of the North or South,
and you fear the decline of man.
Yours was decided like a trampled flag
or a horse ripped open by an unavoidable blow.
You write love poems, tell of dreams
opponents of anguish.
Ah no, underground powers!
You or who? On the Day of Judgement
let his larva dangle
from the thread of a spider newly alive.

LOVE POEM

The wind wavers, ecstatic, bringing
leaves on the trees of the park,
the grass is already around
the walls of the Castle, the sand
barges make way on the Naviglio Grande.
Irritating, unhinged, it is a day
that returns from the cold like any other,
proceeds, wills. But there is you, and you have no limits:
so ravish immovable death
and prepare our bed of living.

I HAVE LOST NOTHING

I am still here, the sun turns
at my shoulder like a hawk and earth
repeats my voice in yours.
Visible time begins again
in the eye that rediscovers light.
I have lost nothing.
To lose is to go beyond
a diagram of the sky
along movements of dreams, a river
full of leaves.

ON THE ISLAND

A hill, the symbols
of time, the mind's mirror
continuous, motionless,
listen to themselves, await
the reply to come. Our hour
goes off without warning, sharpened beam
in the harmonic labyrinth.

It is March, with blue clefts,
the man leaves his bed of leaf-boughs
and goes in search of stone and lime.
He has Lucifer on his hair,
twinkling in the water, in his pocket a measure
of yellow wood, his feet bare,
he knows how to turn curves, eaves,
he squares up, ties in edges, trusses.
Workman and architect, he is alone,
the donkey bears blocks of stone, a lad
breaks them, loosing off sparks. He works
three or four months before the stickiness
of the heat and rains, dawn and dusk.

Of all the hands that raised walls
on the island, Greek hands or Swabian,
hands of Spain, Saracen hands,
walls of the dog-days and of autumn,
of all the nameless and signet-ringed
hands, I see now
those that raised houses
on the sea of Trabia. Vertical lines,
windings of the air bent
by the leaves of acacia and almond trees.

Beyond the houses, down there
among the hares' lentisks, is dead Solunto.
I climbed that hill one morning
with other boys, along
inner silences. I had
yet to invent life.

TO LIGURIA

On your mountains, in the wheel
of youth, I built a road,
high in the chestnut trees;
the navvies heaved boulders
and dislodged vipers in clusters.
It was summer of the meridian
nightingales, of the white lands,
the mouth of the river Roja.
I wrote poems of the darkest
nature of things,
wanting to change the destruction,
searching for love and wisdom
in the solitude of your lonely leaves.
And the mountain and the summer crumbled.
Along the sea, too,
the earth is greedy in Liguria,
as if measured, the gesture
of him who is born on the rocks
of your shores. But if the Ligurian
raises a hand,
he moves it in sign of justice.
Loaded with patience
of all the time of his sadness.
And always the seaman
thrusts the sea far
off from his houses to swell
the land for his son-of-the-waters stride.

IMPERCEPTIBLE TIME

In the garden the orange
reddens, imperceptible
time dances
on its skin,
the mill-wheel breaks loose
at the water's full,
but keeps on turning
and winds a minute
by minute past
or future. Different is
time on the fruit's vortex:
insistent on the body
reflecting death,
slipping contorted,
closing the mind's
hold, writing
a proof of life.

ENOUGH ONE DAY TO BALANCE THE WORLD

Intelligence, death, dream
discredit hope. In this night
at Brașov in the Carpathians, among trees
not mine, I search in time
for a woman of love. Heat splits
the poplar leaves, and I
tell myself words that I do not know,
overturn lands of memory.
Dark jazz, Italian songs
pass upside down on the colour of irises.
In the fountain's roar
your voice is lost:
enough one day to balance the world.

I HAVE FLOWERS AND AT NIGHT
CALL ON THE POPLARS

Sesto S. Giovanni Hospital, November 1965

My shadow is on another hospital
wall. I have flowers and at night
call on the poplars and plane trees of the park,
trees with fallen leaves, not yellow,
near white. The Irish nuns never mention
death, seem moved by the wind, are not
surprised to be young and kind; a vow
freed in the harsh prayers.
I feel like an emigrant who keeps
watch closed up in his blankets,
calm, on the ground. Perhaps I am always dying.
But gladly I listen to the words of life
I have never understood, pause
over long conjectures. Certain, I shall not escape;
I shall be true to life and death,
in body and spirit
in every visible foreseen direction.
At times some light thing overcomes me,
a patient time, the absurd
difference that runs
between death and the illusion
of the heart's beating.

Two Uncollected Poems

LINES TO ANGIOLA MARIA

Rossi, the kind of friend there was
in the time of Catullus
offers you in his languid, elliptical
colours broom flowers
on a boundless surround of air.
He speaks indeed to your lonely life
in a children's place
in the frenzy of dreams, already troubled
over the fate of mankind. Beyond
the trees the window makes tangles of images,
thoughts. Perhaps it moves
over Villa Letizia in a time
of bright moments, swift
as the joy that almost took you,
difficult, almost a law
anchoring pain. And at Villa Letizia
in the land of lakes and rivers,
among people who love the light
not knowing how it shoots from the sky
I looked through the leaves at your hands
as you spoke unerring words.

Perhaps the boys of your far-off schools
and the dusty, changing régimes of thought
that brought no cindery words to your lips,
but visible certainties,
lessons of the soul,
cried out inside you.

225

Your burning hands
were recounting something I heard
in a strange echo
of pain and blood and weeping
for everything lost in love
that I must patiently bear.
Where do we go in our youth?
In memory someone still says:
"For one wreath
that I saw every flower
will make me sigh."
And you who pick out the lines no longer know
whether a boy in a schoolroom, or voice of a loved one,
to you silent mother
of poor ones, rich in spirit.

[This poem was published in a special edition of only five copies
with a reproduction of a painting by Attilio Rossi on 24 October
1965, at the Arti Grafiche Amilcare Pizzi in Milan.]

226

HOW BRIEF THE NIGHT

How brief the night, my love. Already
on your brow a ray of light
and in your Byzantine madonna's hair:
from the caravans along the river
voices of the young nomads,
tightrope walkers in want
and words walled up in contempt
stir ancient roots.
I remember the boy who cast off
his marooned islander's solitude
on Sicily's Bosphorus.
But you wake in your beauty.
Burning and dark you wake me too
to new dizzy heights; restless, bled dry,
you draw me into an unremembering night.
Here perhaps I am living my last life.

[Published in *Corriere della Sera* to commemorate the eightieth
anniversary of the poet's birth. It is claimed in the accompanying
article as, possibly, his last poem, and the date given is August,
1967.]

DISCOURSE ON POETRY

Philosophers, the natural enemies of poets and the inveterate card-indexers of critical thinking, maintain that poetry (and all the arts), like the works of nature, is subject to no change in the course of a war or afterwards. An illusion, because war changes the moral life of a people, and man returning from war finds that the measures of certainty in a mode of inner life are gone, forgotten or belittled during his ordeals with death.

War conscripts by force a latent order in man's thought, a firmer hold on truth. The occasions of reality are carved into its history. Valéry, in 1918, closes a period of French poetry, and Apollinaire opens another, the modern period. D'Annunzio's influence (the poet who consciously sounded the call to battle) crumbles in that very year, and the reaction against his poetic creed and language begins. In 1945 silence descends on the Hermetic school, on the last Florentine pastoral cave of metric phonemics. Since then, "waiting time" has been on trial. Maturity or decadence of a language? Criticism can not answer the question, and attempts to draw up balance sheets and pseudo-histories of poetry between the two wars, indicating its links with a humanist tradition. They are temporary tombstones that one day will be raised to replace the chronicle of formal ashes with the history of contemporary poetic man. One branch of criticism, hardened in methodology that is too abstract, has for more than twenty years evoked "taste" as a touchstone for the recognition of a poem. Steeped in romantic vices, it concerned itself with "form" in order to disentangle itself from Crocean critical tradition. By means of clever distortions (the false "generations" formula, for example) a recent anthology of twentieth-century poetry offers us stiff gallery groups of poets from 1905 to 1945 (from the Crepuscular to the heads and tails of the Hermetics) in a sequence that has verbal life without any systematic coherence.

Hermetic criticism, whose first pink birthday ribbons were tied by Luciano Anceschi, began its first reading exercises, I believe, about 1936, with a study by Oreste Macri on the poetic of the word in my poetry. The philosopher evinced an enthusiasm for the philological approach: perhaps this was the right way, following the lesson of history to reach some conclusions about the origins of today's Italian poetic language. Anceschi attributed the first reactions against d'Annunzio, and the timid articulations of a new *ars poetica* first to Campana, in his *New Poems,* and then to the Crepuscular poets, in an attempt to bring the "fractures" of Ungaretti (of *L'Allegria,* that is, which is not Hermetic) into a traditional line of descent. In doing so he followed the lead of his master, Giuseppe de Robertis. A tempered, baroque perspective of reading leads the critic from these premises to uncertain conclusions, to alarming documents (choice is, indeed, a critical act) on the validity of a concrete, positive poetic period in Italian literary history. The critic who undertook an ambitious examination of the innovators, instead of demonstrating a "semantic of constructions" (of images, to be exact) in order to establish the origins of a Hermetic school – and no one can deny that there was one – returned, for whatever reason, to the abstract geometry of pure art, to a spiritual or stylistically evocative Arcadia within the allowed limits of formal autonomy. In this way there is a marked absence of critical orientation towards recent poetry, the poetry crystallized by the last war, while the exertions of minor critics turned new symbolisms and existential judgements against the silence of the poets. Was it a criticism by emblems, a purely formal criticism? The results disappear in hazy approximations. Here the Crepuscular poets, here the Futurists, and there the poets of *La Voce,* a chronicle that cannot distinguish poetry from literature. The poets, in fact, make their appearance as verifiable motifs of a literary movement, continuing a phase previously interrupted by the "shadow" Corazzini, the semblance Campana, the lemur Sbarbaro. These phantoms insist that many centuries of Italian poetry carry the precious animations of Arcadia; a flourish of voices deadened by the Communes, the Signorias, the Principates, the Courts, the ecclesiastical powers. It is a heritage of analogous encounters in which the poet is the "unloved lover", numbered, punctual as death, between fire and ice. This was the poet, a man of sentimental risks, an inferior nature, uncertain in love that others, all others, by contrast, possess, rich in psychological terminology: in effect, it is this aesthetic and doctrinaire zealousness that in the course of time, from the origins of our literature, salvages seven or eight poets, seven or eight men. So because of its allegiance to traditional procedures, within the narrow limits of what is, except for two or three adequate and communicable examples, mainly a *vox literaria,* this criticism merely prompts the question: Who are these poets, and what do they represent in the contemporary world? Are they playing with shadows in pure forms of art, or do they link literature to life through a development of their understanding and their response to the constraints of time? The critical itinerary is necessary. The war jolted a poetic language that was reaching out towards an involvement with aspects of the earth in order to attain the universal. Allegories were dissolved in the solitude of the dictatorship. But criticism preferred intellectual resolutions of the poetic process: it sought to identify poetic personalities, the existence of the shaping word in symbols and Petrarchan convolutions. But literature "reflects", while poetry "makes". Only *after* his experience as an "irregular" does the poet become a participant in literature. The poet modifies the world with his liberty and truth, by a forced yet natural shattering of metric and technical conventions. Homer's voice is there before Greece, and Homer "forms" the civilization of Greece. "The history of forms as the history of the word" would not, even if complete, exhaust the history of the poets. The poet is a man bound to other men in the field of culture, and is important for his "content" (that is the important word) as well as for his

231

voice, his vocal harmonies, which are instantly recognized when imitated.

The poet does not "say". He takes full account of his own soul and consciousness and makes these secrets of his "exist", forcing them from anonymity to identity. So what are the words of these poets between the two wars? Have they rights, as masters, to citizenship in the contemporary world, or are they pilgrims, serving stylistic operations, worn-out literary modes? No one has spoken out, and many critics writing between the two wars have repeated vague schemes, resemblances rather than images of man. Poetry is man, as I have said: and the filing cards docketed under "taste" are scarcely an introduction to the drama of a part of Italian history, but merely notes for amplification: the logic of fancy, as criticism, can not measure up to poetry, since poetry does not "measure" good innovations, and is committed to truth, not falsehood.

In 1945, formal criticism, empiric, indecisive and unsure in making judgements, was joined by a criticism which, if limited, was realist, and though not yet Marxist, tended towards the orthodox formulations of Marxism. Left in the encyclopedic "limbo" of the various aesthetic trends, the history of poetry between the two wars got down to other, more scientific investigations. We are aware of the dangers of the theoretical machinery of an unsystematized aesthetic – the Marxist aesthetic itself is changing, and the writings of Marx and Engels on art and literature are being interpreted according to the development of contemporary critical thinking – but with the dawn of a new conception of the world, we can look for investigations more concerned with the presence of man.

From 1945 the new generation, reacting against current poetics for the historical reasons given at the opening of this essay, have suddenly found themselves without any apparent leaders to enable them to continue writing poetry. They abandoned the humanist tradition, recognizing its maturity, but not its exclusiveness, and created a literary

232

situation that can only evoke admiration in all who are concerned in the fate of Italian culture.

The search for a new language coincides this time with an impetuous search for man: in effect, the reconstruction of man swindled by war, that "re-making of man" I referred to in 1946, not in a moral sense, because morality cannot constitute poetry. A new poetic language, when another is about to reach maturity, postulates an extreme violence. Formalist criticism (and not only this), confronted with the poetic documents of the new generation, speaks of a "translation style", and deals with the desire for "discourse" in the poetic utterances only from its external aspects – often unmetrical and prosaic.

But does "translation style" imply imitation of foreign spirits and poetics? It is a question that must be clarified. There arises in reaction against the traditional Arcadia, against the contaminated, elegiac, amorous exercises and revived Petrarchism, the first lexicon of a new poetry (the lexicon of poetry between the two wars had been highlighted, through rigorous examination, by Francesco Flora) offering broad movements of rhythm and "forms". Its hexameters may be off-key, in response to the "prescription" of a literary genre, but a social poetry is beginning to flourish, a poetry that concerns itself with the various levels of human society. It is not sociological poetry, because no poet would dream of evoking the power of his soul and intelligence in order to "sociologize". Dante, Petrarch, Foscolo, Leopardi have written social poems, poems that were necessary at a given moment of civilization. But the poetry of the new generation – let us call it social in the sense indicated – aspires to dialogue rather than monologue and constitutes a demand for dramatic poetry, an elementary "form" of theatre. The *Contrasto* of Ciullo d'Alcamo and the *Lamenti* of the Sicilian school exemplify a state of breakaway, in this case from the Provençal school, which, a few poets excepted, was another Arcadia. Perhaps the new poetry can become dramatic or epic, in the modern sense.

233

But, I repeat, not gnomic or sociological. Civil poetry, of course, has deep pitfalls, and has sometimes dallied with "aestheticisms" of a people. One calls to mind Tyrtaeus inviting the young men to fight in the front rank for their country, because the body of an old man is unsightly, while a boy's corpse is always beautiful. The new generation is deeply *engagé* in every sense in the literary field. The new "contents" are heavy, but the content is conditioned by the course of history. The poet of today knows that he can not write lyrical idylls or horoscopes. Fortunately he is not besieged by the pressures of contemporary criticism at his elbow, chivvying him and hinting at more or less probable avenues for poetry to explore, as happened in the previous period; a criticism anticipating poetic solutions, a philosophy ruling over poetry. Hegel wrote that art was dying because it was being caught up in philosophy, in the world of thought. And today it might seem that poetry tends to disappear in the "thought" of poetry.

Returning, however, to that "translation style", the slighting description of the texture of poetry around 1945, we can say that both formalist and historical materialist criticism use the phrase to indicate a "mode", a language taken directly from the translation of foreign poetry. Was it the right term, or was it not, rather, a general approximation concerning a "taste" for speaking of the world and the things of the world using a new technique, foreshadowing a concrete language that would reflect the real, and displace the planes of rhetoric? Our poetic tradition has always seemed to the foreign reader like a dense mass of impenetrable schemes in which man wastes his best moments on elegiac occasions, cut off from the real passions inherent in his nature. After forty years of critical silence on the subject of Italian poetry Europe has begun to read our poems again: not those in the Hermetic tradition, but the ones that ask or answer questions to men, to poems of '43, '44 and '45 and of more recent date. Is this interest due to a projection of feelings and objects that man of today has in common? Is it, therefore, an ethical and problematic kind of attention? I do not believe so. It is, in fact, the "formal" reasons, those least obvious to us now, that open our poetry to human participation in the world. It relates through its poetic commitments, obscured after Leopardi, not because of its linguistic artifacts. It is a sign of an active presence of our civilization, and with it, of Italian man. This is the true tradition, beyond the courtly flutes of nature suppressed in eternal Arcadia. The secret of a poetic language remains long unrevealed to criticism when the model branches away into imitation and its best memory crumbles into a "school". It is then that minor poets offer in the name of beauty pieces of balanced literary craftsmanship superimposed on the repetition of "common" images no longer original. Can man, as he is, be the content of a deterministic poetic? In order to describe the poetic experience of these last years the term "ethical realism" has been used, "real" (or "the truth") referring to the representation itself, and "ethical" to its purpose. It is easy to classify; but through his hostile existence, the harshness of his political mind, his fight against pain, man has drawn closer to man, and the poet to his listener. Sometimes the modern poet is eloquent (ancient persuasive eloquence has a different metaphysical voice) and he seems to communicate with a world drawn together into a limited landscape (his own country): and he is eloquent in spite of his subdued, familiar tone of voice. These are often men from Southern Italy – from Lucania, the Abruzzi, Puglia, the islands – but also from Piedmont and Veneto. From their lowly, feudal heritage they have opened clear, straight dialogues on their fate. They have no childhood nor childhood memory, but chains yet to be broken and solid realities with which to enter the cultural life of the nation. The muses of the woods and valleys are silent in them: their peasant mythologies are filled with the roar of landslides and floods. Some day we shall make a poetic map of the South; and no matter if it still touches Magna Graecia, with its skies looking down over impassive images of innocence and blinding senses. There, perhaps, the "permanence" of poetry is being born. Fortunately there are no highly cultured dialect poets to reduce them to thumbnail sketches, and their syntactic and linguistic "migrations" already support a special lexicon, the announcement of a language. In Tuscany, regrettably, the Guittone d'Arezzos are still to be found, rearing in their precious doctrines the last chimeras of the domains of absence, where the existential lathe revolves. In that other, popular, poetic geography (of little importance, say the critics) the presence of man, his feelings, his gestures, his works, is true. We shall not speak of ethical realism: poets only teach us to live: the material is difficult enough to constrain to new forms. The impulse to break and re-make the hendecasyllabic measure took a generation to conceive and develop. The faculty of rhythmic reading according to traditional metrical writing had been lost. Poets are recognized by their special pronunciation of metrical measures, and their voice (their song) consists of that cadence. Their unit of expression may be metrically long or short, but that "voice" will always be detectable in any structure. There is a voice for every poet, and even in that "translation style", what is important is the poetic pronunciation.

On the subject of the language of the "real", in an essay on Dante I referred to the lasting power of the "simple style". I also noted its intensity, because the language of the *Commedia,* though its real base was the *dolce stil nuovo,* had been purified by contact with its real, human content. The figures of Dante looked towards a drama no longer that of the classical world, though the mode of representing (or inventing) them had its roots there. The lesson of Dante served Petrarch and the major writers of the Cinquecento: it was, indeed, an exalted sign of Italian literary civilization. And it is not only in one direction that today we can read Dante in order to forget Petrarch and his obsessive cadences reflected in the little space assigned to them by the sentiment. Does Dante's social poetry, his "beyond" set in the landscape

236

of the earth still raise doubts, or can it be the "legal" point of departure for the new poets? The "translation style" can surprise anyone accustomed to the special movement of the lyric; but it opens a discourse rare in Italian poetry, and shatters forever harmonious approaches to the Arcadias. Perhaps it will create other rhetorics, but it will free our poetry from servitude now that it has just gained entrance to the literary dominions of European man, cut off, until yesterday, by walls of silence – the same walls that Italian criticism has raised around it. Beyond them, from time to time, criticism seeks out the major writers of the new movement with the ancient aesthetic gauges (not all, however), and only recognizes "contents", judgements, hopes. Dreams are merely sounds of life, cruel replies to the most habitual and worrying questions. And forms? Where is the *dolce color d'oriental zaffiro* ("sweet tint of oriental sapphire"), *la fresca aura dei lauri* ("the cool air of the laurels")?

The two criticisms theorize, and would create the poets in conformity with the limitations of their ideas on art, believing that poetry can be reduced to a science, though they know that then it would be the poet who would force their science to bend to him as an "irregular" by nature.

The grounds of my discourse may seem to be polemical, with reference also to my own situation as a poet, but the documents of the future literary history of the twentieth century (I have culled two typical quotations) are mediocre evidence, catalogues of literary artisanship. Poets – I quote Croce's words – "are little disposed to organic and philosophical considerations, but acute and discriminating on particular questions." So they can discuss the examples offered by anthologists and distinguish, if nothing more, between literature and truth – that is, poetic creation. They can consider the manifestation of the poet in the contemporary world, in his attempt to join life to literature. The art-life relationship is at the centre of the problems of modern thought: but the poet – I have called him elsewhere "imperfection of nature", because he has opened up a dialogue with man – is rejected by the supreme aesthetic orders.

"Chiare, fresche, dolci acque!" ("Clear, cool, sweet waters!") If only these were times for such fond murmurings, and the poetic vision of the past still potent enough to re-see the world in their gentle measures and sentiments. Here, today, the present generation that dares to read new numbers in the tables of poetry learns day by day what it means to write poetry – so easy before the civil and political upheavals. Gramsci, from the darkness of his prison, saw with clear eyes the "literary" principles of the world. The position of the poet can not be passive in society: he modifies the world, as we have said. His powerful images, the ones he creates, beat more than philosophy or history on man's heart. Poetry is transformed into ethics precisely because of the beauty it renders: its responsibility is in direct proportion to its perfection. To write poetry involves being judged: the aesthetic judgement is intrinsic to the social reactions a poem evokes. We are aware of the reservations that must modify such claims. But a poet is a poet when he does not renounce his presence in a given land, at the right time, politically defined. And poetry is liberty and truth in that time, not abstract modulations of sentiment.

It is absurd for criticism to put "waiting time" on trial today, in a period of poetic development; above all when new theories are emerging, and the continuation of an outworn poetic may convey a sense of "duration". The war has interrupted a culture and proposed new values for man; and though the arms have so far remained hidden away, the dialogue of the poets with men is more necessary than science and international agreements, which can be betrayed. Italian poetry after 1945 is, by its nature, choral; it flows with broad rhythms, speaks of the real world with common words; occasionally it aspires to epic. Because it has opened itself to forms that deny the false Italian tradition it has a difficult way ahead. Its poets, for the present, pay out the silence amid political alarms, and the chronicles of moral decadence.

[First published as an appendix to *The False and True Green*.]

EPILOGUE: TO SALVATORE QUASIMODO

You have lost nothing,
because you were always dying,
listening to words of a life
you never understood,
the patient time
between death and the illusion
of the heart's beating.

On a page of the eighteen times re-written
Catullus you made a home for in the tongue
you made fit for Callimachus too, and sent
me only a week ago, sadly I write
Thànatos athànatos:
sole certainty
of a Greek Sicilian.

JACK BEVAN
Summer, 1968

BIBLIOGRAPHY

QUASIMODO IN ENGLISH TRANSLATION

Allen Mandelbaum, ed. and trans., *The Selected Writings of Salvatore Quasimodo*, bilingual edition, New York, 1960

Thomas G. Bergin and Sergio Pacifici, trans., *The Poet and The Politician, and other essays*, Carbondale, Illinois, 1964

Jack Bevan, ed. and trans., *Selected Poems*, Harmondsworth, 1965

Edith Farnsworth, trans., *To Give and To Have, and other poems*, bilingual edition, Chicago, 1969

Jack Bevan, trans., *Debit and Credit*, London, 1972

CRITICAL ESSAYS ON QUASIMODO

C. M. Bowra, "An Italian Poet: S. Quasimodo", *Horizon* vol. XVI, London, 1947

Allen Mandelbaum, "I Migliori Fabbri: Quasimodo", *Inventario*, May–December 1954

J. M. Cohen, *Poetry of This Age*, London, 1959

G. Gambon, "A Deep Wind: Quasimodo's 'Tindari'", *Italian Quarterly* vol. III no. 2, New Brunswick, 1959

Sergio Pacifici, "Salvatore Quasimodo, Nobel Prize for Literature 1959", *Saturday Review*, New York, 7 November 1959

C. A. McCormick, "S. Quas'modo and the Struggle against Silence", *Meanjin Quarterly*, Melbourne, 1961

F. J. Jones, "The Poetry of S. Quasimodo", *Italian Studies* vol. XVI, Cambridge, 1961

Sergio Pacifici, *A Guide to Contemporary Italian Literature*, New York, 1962

G. Finzi, ed., *Quasimodo e la critica*, Milan, 1969
(a collection of international criticism, in Italian)

INDEX OF TITLES

A Copper Amphora 178
Again a Green River 122
Again I Hear the Sea 139
Alien City 100
Alleyway 41
Almost a Madrigal 149
Almost an Epigram 187
Along the Isar 207
Amen for Sunday in Albis 82
An Act or a Name of the Spirit 182
An Answer 196
An Open Arc 177
The Ànapo 88
Ancient Winter 36
And Suddenly It's Evening 29
And Your Dress Is White 32
The Angel 70
Angels 31
Anno Domini MCMXLVII 150
Another Answer 197
Apollyon 87
Aries 33
At Night on the Acropolis 189
Auschwitz 166
Autumn 61

Beach at St Antiochus 123
Become Darkness and Height 73
Before the Statue of Ilaria del
    Carreto 109
Beyond the Waves of the Hills 161
Birth of Song 50
By the Adda 138

Came Down to Me Through New
    Innocence 65
Cape Caliakra 211
Changeful with Stars and Quiet 72
Colour of Rain and Iron 148
Convalescence 69
Cool Seashore 39

Day after Day 130
Day Stoops 35
The Dead 37
The Dead Guitars 157

Dead Heron 89
Deadwater 34
Debit and Credit 203
Delphi 192
Delphic Woman 119
Dialogue 147

Earth 34
Elegos for the Dancer Cumani 118
Elegy 139
Eleusis 194
Enemy of Death 158
Enough One Day to Balance the
    World 223
Epitaph for Bice Donetti 146
The Eucalyptus 48
Even My Company Forsakes Me 43
Evening in the Màsino Valley 116
Every Form Waylost in Me 44

The False and True Green 159
The Ferry 140
First Day 76
Following the Alpheus 191
For My Mortal Smell 98
Fortress of Bergamo Alta 137
From Disfigured Nature 176
From the Shores of the Balaton 208
From the Web of Gold 170

The Gentle Hill 107
Give Me My Day 68
Glendalough 213
Greedily I Spread My Hand 41
Green Drift 77

Hermaphrodite Earthworm 79
Hidden Life 71
Homecomings 42
Horses of Moon and Volcanoes 121
How Brief the Night 227
How Long the Night 161

I Have Flowers and at Night Call
    on the Poplars 224
I Have Lost Nothing 218

241

Imitation of Joy 120
Imperceptible Time 222
In a Distant City 160
In Chiswick Cemetery 215
In Light of Skies 97
In the Ancient Light of the Tides 52
In the Feeling of Death 101
In the Right Human Time 99
In This City 184
In Your Light I Am Wrecked 91
The Incomparable Earth 174
Inscription for the Fallen of
    Marzabotto 198
Inscription for the Partisans of
    Valenza 199
Insomnia 92
Island 66
Island of Ulysses 94

Lament for the South 145
Lament of a Friar in an Icon 58
Laude (29 April 1945) 164
Letter 128
Letter to My Mother 153
Lesser Curve 55
Lines to Angiola Maria 225
Living I Sicken 81
Love Poem 218

The Magpie Laughs Black in the
    Orange Trees 105
Man of My Time 142
Marathon 193
The Maya at Mérida 216
The Meagre Flower Is Already
    Flying 124
Metamorphoses in the Saint's Urn 64
Milan, August 1943 132
Minotaur at Knossos 193
Mirror 39
Mouth of the River Roja 61
Mycenae 190
My Country Is Italy 151
My Patient Day 63

Near a Saracen Tower, for My Dead
    Brother 162
The Negro Church at Harlem 210
News Item 186

Night Birds' Refuge 43
19 January 1944 129
No Night So Clear Ever
    Vanquished You 38
No One 40
Now Day Is Breaking 110

O My Gentle Beasts 134
Of Another Lazarus 140
Of the Sinner of Myths 102
Often a Coastland 93
On the Banks of the Lambro 114
On the Hill of the "Terre Bianche" 90
On the Island 219
On the Willow Boughs 127
One Buried in Me Declares 56
One Evening, Snow 111
Only if Love Should Pierce You 205

Perhaps the Heart 131
Piazza Fontana 112
Playmate 57
Prayer to the Rain 60

Quarries 98

The Rain Is Already With Us 110
Rest of the Grass 51
Roads of Rivers in Sleep 78

Salt-Bed in Winter 95
Sardinia 96
Seed 75
A September Night 206
The Silence Does Not Deceive
    Me 212
Snow 130
Soldiers Weep by Night 188
Song of Apollyon 86
Sorrow of Things I Do Not
    Know 36
Space 35
Still of Hell 185
Street in Agrigentum 106
Suffered Forms of Trees 80
Sunken Oboe 47
Syllables to Erato 85

The Tall Sailing Ship 113

242

Temple of Zeus at Agrigentum 163
Thànatos Athànatos 152
There Was a Sound of Airy Seasons
   Passing 37
This Pilgrim 136
Threshold of Puberty 124
To a Hostile Poet 170
To Liguria 221
To My Father 179
To My Land 49
To Night 63
To the Cervi Brothers, to Their
   Italy 168
To the Fifteen of Piazzale Loreto 165
To the New Moon 195
Today, the Twenty-First of
   March 175
Tollbridge 209
The Tombs of the Scaligers 181
Tree 33
Tuscan Crossbowmen 214

Varvàra Alexandrovna 204
Visible, Invisible 173

The Wall 133
The Wall 183
Water Decomposes Dormice 74
What Is It, Shepherd of Air? 108
Where the Dead Stand Open-Eyed 67
Wind at Tindari 30
Winter Night 132
Without Memory of Death 59
Woods Sleep 62
Word 53
Words to a Spy 217
Written, Perhaps, on a Tomb 135

You Call on a Life 38
Young Woman Lying Back in the
   Midst of the Flowers 54
Your Silent Foot 141

243

INDEX OF FIRST LINES

A dry birch branch with the
    green 204
A happy wafting of winged 92
A hill, the symbols 219
A plant, neither laurel 192
A sun breaks swollen in sleep 49
A tangle of black and white roots 36
A wry smile cut your face 37
Again I am ravaged by a green
    river 122
Against you they are raising
    a wall 183
Along the Bulgarian Dobruja
    on clay 211
Already on the stadium wall 133
And again the winter night 132
And if delight in me overwhelms
    you 72
And we, how could we sing 127
Another hour falls 100
Another foreign city: the evening
    crumbling 207
At Balatonfüred a young lime
    tree 208
"At cantu commotae Erebi de
    sedibus imis 147
At dayrise lit by the moon 96
At Eleusis a general has erected 194
At your banks I hear dove water 88

But what for the love of Christ do
    you want? 197
By your side at noon the Adda
    strains along 138

Claude Vivier and Jacques
    Sermeus 186
Clear dawn of funeral window-
    panes 74
Closed water, sleep of the marshes 34
Cold harbinger of night 139
Convalescence 69

Day after day: damned words, and
    the blood 130
Dear one, you should not 158

Delay your favour, grasping pain 47
Desire of your bright 36
Do not forget that you live in the
    midst of the animals 205
Dressed up in gay brocades the
    bowmen 214
Drift of light: changing
    whirlpools 51
Dry womb of love and young 62

Each of us is alone on the heart
    of the earth 29
Esposito, Fiorani, Fogagnolo 165
Even my company forsakes me 43
Evening falls: again you leave us 130
Evening shatters in the earth 177
Evening: sorrowing light 77

Far from the Vistula, along the
    northern plain 166
Far-off behind closed doors,
    I hear 111
Far-off birds, open in the evening 107
From farthest winters the
    thunder's 140
From the pools blessed clouds
    arise 97
From the web of gold foul spiders
    hang 170
From where are you calling? The
    fog 140
From you a shadow melts 33
From your womb 63

Garbled, the beating 212
Give me my day 68

Her eyes to the rain and spirits of
    the night 146
Here, far from everyone 135
Here is the sea, the agave flowering
    already 141
Heroes now are fossils, debated 181
High up stands a twisted pine 43
How brief the night, my love.
    Already 227

How long the night, the moon pink and green 161

I am born in your shipwrecking light 91
I am closed in a dark 35
I am perhaps a child 40
I am still here, the sun turns 218
I banish myself; shadow 56
I compare my man's life to you 39
I do not know what light you gave me 57
I feel another death unknown to me 69
I find you in the happy landing-places 78
I happily breathe on a root 81
I have long owed you words of love 174
I held a gleaming 162
I live in great drought 58
I read you the soft verses of antiquity 129
In all parts of the earth base minds are sniggering 168
In killed trees 98
In poverty of flesh I am here 41
In the air of moon cedars 119
In the beginning God created the heaven 195
In the clay's bile 123
In the garden the orange 222
In the lazy moving of skies 33
In the spaces of the hills 116
In the warm swamp, driven into the mud 89
In the wind of deep light she lies 99
In this city there is even a machine 184
In vain you search in the dust 132
Island city 52
Islands that were my home 121
It is not through intrigue, hybrid 161
It seemed as if voices were raised 37
Intelligence, death, dream 223

Languor of love, sadness 38
Look! on the trunk 39

Lose me, Lord, that I may not hear 55
Lost to you all sweetness in life 31
Love of you, my land 66

Many nights now I have heard the sound of the sea 139
"Mater dulcissima, now the mists are descending 153
Mild autumn, I possess myself 61
Mild torpor of waters 79
Mother, why do you spit at a corpse 164
My land is on the rivers, hugs the sea 157
My patient day 63
My shadow is on another hospital 224

Neither the Cross, nor childhood, the scourge 188
Night is ended and the moon 110
Night, serene shades 34
No night so clear ever vanquished you 38
No sweetness ripens me 48
Not from the sky, but steeply down 160
Nothing, you give me nothing, you 203
Now autumn mars the green of hills 134
Now light matures, first fruit of the sun 80
Now under a tender moon, your hills 109

Of my life I shall know nothing 124
Of the sinner of myths 102
Often a coastland 93
On the hedge the thorns 178
On the Mycenae road with its eucalyptus 190
On the straw-coloured sands of Gela 170
On your mountains, in the wheel 221
One could sense the secret season 54
One night at Athens in the white sea 189

Other life held me: alone 44
Outlasting the day 90

Peace of spreading waters 76
Perhaps it is a true sign of life 105
Piazza Navona, in the dark I lay 42
Pirate life, you have raised the grand
    ensign 182
Plunderer of languors and pains 124

Resonances of myrtles 215
Rossi, the kind of friend there
    was 225

Sky-blue trees 101
So, I return to the silent square 136
So shall we have to deny you,
    God 152
Sometimes your voices call me
    back 41
Space and the hour strain on 71
Spring raises trees and rivers 59
Stilled is the ancient voice 94
Sweetness you never rest in me 95
Syllables of shadows and leaves 98

Tang of the sky 60
Terrestrial night, I was pleased
    sometimes 86
That day vanished from us
    unblemished 114
The angel sleeps 70
The contortionist in the bar, a
    melancholy 187
The dead mellow 64
The dead of Glendalough 213
The deep brasses of the wind 61
The girl who is sitting on the grass
    lifts 163
The harmonies of the earth 191
The lament of the mothers at
    Marathon 193
The loved wind lingers
    no more 112
The more the days disperse far
    off 151
The mountains lie inert 87
The negro church at Harlem 210
The rain at Mérida falls hot 216

The rain is already with us 110
The red moon, the wind, your 145
The sharp smell of the limes will
    drown 131
The sunflower bends to the west 149
The symmetrical leaf 176
The wind of the woods 118
The wind is still there that I
    remember 106
The wind wavers, ecstatic,
    bringing 218
The young Cretans had slim 193
There again, the call of the
    ancient 108
There is a spy who writes 217
This is a memorial to blood 198
This silence that hangs in the
    streets 128
This stone 199
Though the anchor of Ulysses
    burns in the mind 196
"Timor mortis conturbat me"? 206
Tindari, I know you gentle 30
To a saltpetre sun grey with
    mistral 209
To you the heart in solitude bends 85
Today, the twenty-first of March,
    the Ram 175
Tonight your voice came down
    to me 65
Trees of shadows 75

Visible, invisible 173

Water-spring: light reappearing 50
We shall follow silent houses 67
When birds came stirring the
    leaves 113
Where Messina was on the violet 179
Where trees deepen 120

You are still the one with stone and
    sling 142
You come into my voice 73
You find me forsaken, Lord 35
You have bent your head, are
    looking at me 32
You have heard the cock crow in the
    air 137

246

You have not betrayed me, Lord 82
You have stopped beating the
   drums 150
You laugh at me, flaying myself for
   words 53

You said: death, silence, solitude 148
You wait for me no more with the
   paltry heart 159
You will not tell us, one night,
   shouting 185